DEATH
on the
DEVIL'S
TEETH

DEATH
on the
DEVIL'S TEETH

THE STRANGE MURDER THAT SHOCKED SUBURBAN NEW JERSEY

JESSE P. POLLACK & MARK MORAN

THE
History
PRESS

Published by The History Press
Charleston, SC 29403
www.historypress.net

Copyright © 2015 by Jesse P. Pollack & Mark Moran
All rights reserved

First published 2015

Manufactured in the United States

ISBN 978.1.62619.628.5

Library of Congress Control Number: 2015937834

For my family—my reason to believe.
—*J.P.*

For the friends and family of Jeannette DePalma, along with the people of New Jersey who offered their help to the authors in the writing of this book so that her story could be told and so that she would not be forgotten.
—*M.M.*

The truth, when you finally chase it down, is almost always far worse than your darkest visions and fears.
—Dr. Hunter S. Thompson (1937–2005)

CONTENTS

PREFACE

The murder of Jeannette DePalma is one of the most bizarre and controversial homicide cases on record, and yet it is largely unknown outside the state of New Jersey. Many postulate that this was by design. Rumors of a nefarious coverup in this case originated only days after Jeannette's body was found on top of a cliff, surrounded by supposed "occult objects." If one side is to be believed, the teenager was one of the first victims of ritual occult murder in suburban America. If the other is taken, this case could be one of the earliest examples of "Satanic panic," decades before the infamous West Memphis Three case.

The story vanished from the newspapers only two weeks after Jeannette's body was discovered, but memories of the girl's death stayed fresh in the gossip of New Jersey residents for years to come. It seemed likely that this was where the story of Jeannette DePalma would remain—dying with those who knew her personally. However, in 1998, the offices of *Weird NJ* magazine received a letter regarding an "alleged ritual human sacrifice" in Springfield's Houdaille Quarry. The letter's author was unsure whether this "sacrifice" actually occurred or was purely myth, but the publication of his vague memory led to a rebirth of interest in this cold case.

A few short years after the letter's appearance in *Weird NJ*, I started writing short pieces for the magazine. A decade would pass, however, before I began researching the case for this book. Leading up to this point, my co-author, *Weird NJ*'s co-founder Mark Moran, worked diligently to bring as many facts as possible about Jeannette's murder to light, conducting interviews with her friends and family and sifting through dozens of letters regarding the case—nearly all of which were mailed anonymously. Eventually, Mark hit a dead end, and the trail again went cold.

I became familiar with Jeannette DePalma and the circumstances surrounding her murder in early 2012 while flipping through back issues of *Weird NJ*. In Issue #22, I found several pages devoted to the case, and I could not shake from my mind the mysterious death of this young woman. I began searching reel after reel of microfilm for articles about this supposed victim of murderous cult members. I then located the surviving investigators who had worked Jeannette's case. Many were willing to speak on the record with me; others were less than enthusiastic, to say the least. I also tracked down many of Jeannette's friends, along with members of the DePalma family, spending countless hours meeting with them and conducting interviews. It soon became apparent that, despite the many years that had passed since the teenager's death, a multitude of her friends and acquaintances were still terrified of whoever was responsible for the horrible act. A significant number of these people would speak to me only under the strict condition of anonymity. This required certain names to be changed within the text. These names are marked with asterisks.

Armed with a wealth of new information about the case, Mark and I decided to team up and write the definitive account of this incredibly strange cold case. A lot of the evidence that we have found is controversial, to say the least, and sometimes contradictory. We have done our absolute best to separate myth from fact wherever possible, all while objectively presenting the many sides of this captivating story. We can only hope that this book will lead to a better understanding of the senseless murder of a young woman and the bizarre events that led up to that dark day in August 1972. Even stranger events surrounding this crime continue to unfold today. The key to finally solving this cold case may lie within these pages. Only time will tell.

JESSE P. POLLACK
February 2015

As a writer for the magazine *Weird NJ*, I am always on the lookout for new, unusual stories to tell. Back around 2002, the publication began receiving vague and anonymous letters about a grisly murder that had taken place some thirty years prior. My curiosity was sparked, and I decided to piece together as many of the facts of the cold case as I could find. That task, as I soon would discover, would be a much more daunting challenge than I ever could have foreseen.

The all-but-forgotten unsolved case began in 1972, when the body of a teenage girl was discovered atop a cliff, high above an abandoned quarry in the township of Springfield, New Jersey. The corpse was found thanks to a dog that had brought home to its master a badly decomposed human forearm. The arm, along with the corpse, would later be identified as having belonged to Jeannette DePalma, a local teenager who had been missing for six weeks.

The details that first drew me to the sad story of Jeannette were the lingering rumors around Union County alleging that the disappearance and subsequent murder had ritualistic overtones. The remote hilltop location where the body was discovered was said to have been strewn with cult-related symbols, and the body of the young girl was rumored to have been placed on a makeshift altar in the woods.

The various versions of the Jeannette DePalma story that I heard blamed either a coven of witches or a local group of Satanists who had sacrificed her. The strangest thing that I encountered in my investigation of the mystery was that after more than thirty years, most people who remembered the crime were still too frightened to speak about it. Everyone I questioned about the murder seemed to recall the same scant and gruesome details, but nobody wanted to go on record or have his or her name published in my article—including members of the Springfield Police Department.

The general consensus of the people I interviewed in regard to Jeannette's murder seemed to agree on certain points: that the killing was in some way cult related, that the Springfield Police Department had covered up certain facts of the case and that Jeannette's killers were most likely still at large. They also shared the desire to see the killer or killers brought to justice so that Jeannette might finally rest in peace.

Aside from her life, the only thing taken from Jeannette DePalma on that lonely, desolate mountaintop in 1972 was a gold cross that she always wore around her neck. The necklace was never found. Back at her home, Jeannette's bedroom was decorated with all manner of religious symbols and posters. One poster bore a picture of Jesus Christ and proclaimed, "You shall know the truth and the truth shall set you free."

Hopefully through this book, the truth will become a little more known, and Jeannette and all those who mourn her shall finally be set free.

MARK MORAN
February 2015

ACKNOWLEDGEMENTS

W̲e would like to thank our families for their constant support and encouragement throughout the creation of this work. We would also like to thank: Wheeler Antabanez, Doyle Argene, Joanne M. Austin, Cheryl Bancey, Darlene Bancey, Gabe Bancey, Margaret Bandrowski, Sonia Leonardo Baxter, Melissa Benner, Elaine Bennett, John Brinton, X-Ray Burns, Edward Cardinal Jr., Edward Cardinal Sr., Russell Christiana, Hugh Curtis, Curtis Dady, Jonathan de la Rosa, Cindy DePalma, Gwendolyn DePalma, Susan DiFrancesco, Grace Petrilli DiMuro, Len Doland, Gail Donohue, John Douglas, Lois Duncan, Nia Eaton, Kristine Mintel Esposito, Jamie E. Farrell, Susan Fensten, Jim Goad, Ashley Gomes, Billy Gregg, Daniel Gregg, William Gregg, Jonathan Grioli, Bill Griswold, Peter Hammer, Michael Helbing, Tom Hunter, Professor Ronald Hutton, Lauren Irene, Nicholas Johnson, Daniel Oxford Jones, Glen Jones, Lee Kimble, Edward Kisch, Curt Knoth, Dylan Knoth, Deborah Kooperstein, Orin Kramer, Dr. Sari Kramer, Wendy Kriss, Molly Hammett Kronberg, Whitney Tarella Landis, Erik Larson, Dan Lurie, Mary Marshall, Christina Mathews, Robert McCarthy, Jill Meier, Dr. Judy Melinek, Michael Mitzner, Bert Model, Eric Model, Audrey Knoth Muratore, Eric Myers, William Nelson, the family of Dominick Olivo, Diane Pezzuti, Rhyin Polen, Nancy Pryor, Kevin Ranoldo, Jerome Rice, Donna Rivera, Deborah Rodriguez, Rai Rothspan, Sal Rubiano, Leslie Rule, Racheal Sajeski, Mark Sceurman, Art Schwartz, Donald Schwerdt, Donald Schwerdt Jr., Heather Shade, Roy Simpson, Judith Small, Marjorie Lange Sportes, Rusty Tagliareni, James Tate, Wayne

Tate, Michael A. Vaccaro, Sandy VanderMeer, Jeffrey Villasenor, Rue Volley, Katherine Weber-Turcotte, Dr. Cyril Wecht, Kyle J. Zalinsky, Nick Zavolas, the Baltusrol Golf Club, the Coldwater Ohio Public Library, the Elizabeth New Jersey Public Library, everyone over at WFMU, the Maplewood Police Department, the Springfield Historical Society, the South Orange Police Department, the Woodbridge New Jersey Public Library and everyone else who lent their encouragement and assistance along the way.

SEPTEMBER 2002

Midday traffic along Route 1's Central New Jersey corridor can be a real nuisance, even if you are not already on a tight schedule with a laundry list of things to do. For Mark Moran and Mark Sceurman, however, this was becoming routine. In less than a decade, their magazine, *Weird NJ*, rose from being an obscure, typewritten newsletter to one of the country's most popular underground publications.

Nine years prior, Moran was a frustrated thirty-year-old graphic designer looking for a way out of his job at a pajama company. This way out would come to him via the turn of a radio dial. One day in 1993, Moran was listening to the legendary New Jersey radio station WFMU. On air was a thirty-six-year-old writer named Mark Sceurman. Moran's attention was immediately drawn to WFMU's Bill Suggs and Andy Breckman interviewing Sceurman about his homemade newsletter. Hand typed and hand stapled, this up-and-coming newsletter featured stories about some of New Jersey's more infamous landmarks and legends—places like Verona's abandoned Essex Mountain Sanatorium and the fabled Albino Village of Clifton. When Moran was not doing silkscreen work at the pajama company, he was out and about photographing similar haunts and attractions. To Moran, Sceurman sounded like a kindred spirit. Reaching for a piece of paper and a pen, Moran decided to reach out to Sceurman, asking for a copy of the newsletter. He also included some of his photography and an illustration of the Jersey Devil.

Moran's letter was the fifty-second piece of correspondence that Sceurman received regarding *Weird NJ*, and he was impressed by the ominous tone of the graphic designer's work. He picked up his phone and dialed Moran, asking if Moran would like to accompany him on a road trip. After a day spent visiting numerous New Jersey attractions, the two decided to stop at the Franklin Tavern in West Orange. While discussing the day's trip over drinks, Sceurman hit Moran with a surprise question: "Would you like to co-publish *Weird NJ* with me?" Blindsided, Moran happily obliged.

Once this partnership was formed, Moran and Sceurman took the handmade newsletter that was only occasionally distributed and transformed it into a professionally printed biannual release. The response was nearly instantaneous and overwhelmingly positive. Moran and Sceurman had found a way to tap into a niche market that was desperately waiting to be explored. Nine years and fifteen issues later, *Weird NJ* had become one of America's most beloved publications, and the magazine was on top of its game.

For these two writers, known to their fans as "The Marks," this particular day in the autumn of 2002 was a "road day." A "road day" was one of the few days out of the year that was not spent sifting through hundreds upon thousands of letters and e-mails, collecting content for what they affectionately called "the 'zine." It was also one of the few days that would not be spent sitting in front of a computer screen for hours on end, designing and editing the layout of the upcoming issue. There were worse things for Moran and Sceurman than sitting in bumper-to-bumper traffic on a mild September day.

Eventually, the two were able to advance far enough to pull into the parking lot of their destination—one of many shops in the area that stocked *Weird NJ* magazine. The Marks opened the trunk, and each grabbed a large cardboard box filled with dozens of fresh copies of the latest issue, #19. The painted image of a devil's face graced its cover, an example of outsider art known to the residents of Boonton Township as "Mr. Kincaid's Nightmare."

The bell above the shop's door jingled as Moran and Sceurman entered. The two set down their boxes and exchanged pleasantries with the store's owner. After a few minutes of small talk, the three men made their way to the rear office of the store to settle their accounts for that half of the year. Sitting at his cluttered desk, the shop owner quickly went over some numbers. Once the total was figured out, the owner cut a check to the Marks for the previous shipment of magazines. Moran and Sceurman shook the owner's hand, and the three began to make their way back toward the front entrance of the store.

Looking over his shoulder, Moran waved to the shop's owner. "So long," he said. "Let us know if you hear about anything weird!" This had become his go-to parting line. Most often, this expression would be met with a friendly chuckle or an enthusiastic "You bet!"

Today would be different.

As Moran made his way out the door, the shop's owner said, "You know, there was one thing…" Moran stopped and turned toward the man. The owner paused. A pensive look came across his face. Moran could tell that this man quickly wished that he had never opened his mouth. Another moment passed. Finally, the shop's owner spoke. "Did you guys ever hear the story of Jeannette DePalma?" he asked, his voice nearly a whisper. "It was some kind of ritual cult killing…"

1

DISCOVERY

Hell is empty. And all the devils are here.
—William Shakespeare, The Tempest

For Patrolman Donald Schwerdt, September 19, 1972, should have been a normal Tuesday. It was his second day back to work after a relaxing vacation, and he was easily beginning to settle back into his routine. Sitting in his modest, two-story home on Brook Street, Schwerdt ate his breakfast and drank his coffee. He then put on his freshly ironed uniform and walked out the door. He was immediately greeted by the smell of honeysuckle and the rumble of approaching school buses. On many days like this one, Schwerdt could be seen making the three-minute walk to work, his seven adoring children following behind like ducks in a row. The five Schwerdt daughters and two Schwerdt sons would almost always meet their father halfway home at the end of his shift, asking how his day went. The forty-four-year-old patrol officer was a late addition to the police department, having spent most of his adult life in the United States Navy and, later, working for the U.S. Postal Service. Despite being one of the oldest officers of his rank, Donald Schwerdt loved being a cop. The pride that he took in his job could be seen in the certain swagger in his walk, his head always held high and his eight-point hat cocked slightly to the side.

Entering the three-story, brick-and-mortar municipal building, Donald Schwerdt made his way into police headquarters, which was housed in the center of the first floor. After reviewing a list of the community's stolen

Donald Schwerdt Sr. pictured in the 1980s. *Courtesy of Donald Schwerdt Sr. and family.*

vehicles, Schwerdt was assigned to patrol the north side of the township. Firing up his patrol car, a late-model Plymouth Fury recently purchased from Morris Avenue Motors, Schwerdt prepared for what he thought would be just another day spent patrolling the streets of the sleepy mountain community of suburban Springfield, New Jersey. It would have never crossed his mind that events were about to unfold that would cast doubt on the police force, divide whole families and terrify the entire tri-state area.

As Schwerdt's patrol car cruised up and down the pristine streets of Springfield, a dog was weaving its way through the labyrinth of trees bordering the nearby Houdaille Quarry. In its mouth, the dog held a decaying human arm.

The canine made its way out of the woods, crossed Mountview and Shunpike Roads and came to rest on the lawn of the brand-new Baltusrol Gardens apartment complex on Wilson Road. The dog loosened its bite, and the arm fell to the ground in front of a row of bushes just outside the rear entrance to the two-story, red brick–clad complex. The glass-paneled front door opened. The dog's owner, a tenant of the building, motioned for her pet to come back inside, completely oblivious to the gruesome souvenir lying only feet away. That discovery would be left for the building's elderly superintendent. Only moments after the dog's return, the superintendent

Springfield's Mountview Road. *Photo by Jesse P. Pollack.*

stepped outside and made her way down six concrete steps to the lawn. Her attention was immediately drawn to something strange resting at her feet.

A scream pierced the mountain air.

"The call came in around eleven o'clock," Schwerdt recalls. "Dispatch radioed me that this woman had found an arm on the lawn of the apartment complex where she lived." Schwerdt's first impression was that the woman was simply the unwitting victim of a practical joke.

"I honestly thought it was a prank," Schwerdt says. "I figured it was going to be a mannequin's arm because this lady was always being harassed by a few of the kids that lived in the apartment complex. They would do things like throw her trash all over the lawn. They were just awful to her. So when I got the call, I figured it was those kids again, and maybe they poured some ketchup on a mannequin arm or something."

There was a slight squeal of the tires and then the throaty moan of the Plymouth Fury's four-barrel carburetor as Schwerdt turned around and headed for Wilson Road. Passing the abandoned Springfield Swim Club, he made his way up the mountain on Shunpike Road. As Schwerdt approached the block of apartments, the tree line quickly began to envelope him, blocking out much of the sunlight. Had he been a superstitious man, Schwerdt might have taken this as an omen. He parked his patrol car in the small lot on Wilson Road and made his way toward the rear of the unfinished

The rear of the Baltusrol Gardens apartment complex. Jeannette DePalma's arm was discovered by the building's superintendent just beyond the bushes to the left. *Photo by Michael Vaccaro.*

apartment complex, his polished shoes glistening in the early afternoon sun as they clicked against the asphalt. As he got closer to the gruesome item in question, Schwerdt quickly discovered that his original assumption was far from true. "When I got there, the arm was lying in the grass," he recalls. "I looked at it, and I said to myself, 'This is human.' I could see the fingernails and the color of the skin." Schwerdt immediately grabbed his camera and took several photographs of the forearm. "I could tell that the arm had been out in the elements for a while. The flesh was real leathery, and it was a sort of maroonish red in color."

Once Schwerdt finished taking photographs, he returned to his patrol car. Clutching his radio's handheld microphone, Schwerdt called out to dispatch. "You better send the detectives up," he said. "We got an arm here, and it's no joke."

Patrolmen Edward Kisch and Dominick Olivo heard this call over their radios and immediately raced to the apartments to provide backup. Fellow officers described Kisch as having good intentions and being very serious about his work. Today, fellow retirees remember the then-thirty-year-old officer for being able to mind his own business and do his job well. The same retirees remember Olivo affectionately as "Dom." In his later years, the robust patrolman reminded some of his colleagues of actor Erik Estrada's portrayal of Officer Frank "Ponch" Poncherello on the hit NBC television drama *CHiPS*.

Once Kisch and Olivo arrived at the apartments, Schwerdt returned to the elderly superintendent and asked how the arm had ended up on the lawn. The superintendent told the officer that her dog had most likely brought it home. Schwerdt asked if he could have a look at her dog, and the superintendent nodded, asking him to follow her to her apartment. There, Schwerdt made a surprising discovery. "The lady brought me over to a puppy—and I mean a *tiny* puppy. That really threw me off. There was no way that this little thing could have brought that arm home." He then proceeded to knock on each door of the apartment complex, asking the tenants if they had any pets. Eventually, Schwerdt found one resident who owned a large Dalmatian. "The tenant told me that she had let her dog out to run earlier that morning, and we determined that this Dalmatian had most likely brought the arm home from wherever it had been roaming."

Standing next to Kisch, Olivo stared at the rotting forearm lying on the ground. After pausing for a moment, the thirty-two-year-old officer felt uneasiness in his stomach. Turning to face Kisch, Olivo remarked, "I think this could be Jeannette DePalma."

"Why do you say that?" Kisch asked.

"Ed, she's the only missing person we've got in town. She's listed as a runaway."

Kisch nodded.

Once a satisfactory number of photographs of the forearm had been taken and the surrounding area had been examined, Kisch placed the detached extremity in a cardboard box and drove it back to the municipal building, where it would wait until the rest of the body could be located.

Back at the Baltusrol Gardens apartment complex, members of Springfield's Detective Bureau had begun to arrive on the scene. Schwerdt and Olivo were instructed to resume their regular patrol duties, while George Parsell, Springfield's chief of police, began coordinating with his detectives to conduct a search for the rest of the remains. The fifty-year-old police chief, described as a huge and lumbering man of few words, made the decision to borrow a bloodhound from the Ocean County Sheriff's Office for use during the planned search. Approximately four hours after the initial discovery of the forearm, the search party was organized and ready to go.

"My shift ended at three o'clock," Schwerdt remembers. "After that, I went home, changed my clothes and we all met back at police headquarters.

We had the Union County Prosecutor's Office, the Ocean County Sheriff's Department with a bloodhound and our group of men. It was decided that we better have a search party check the roadbed of Interstate 78, which was just being built at the time. It was only dirt."

"Basically, all of us were dispatched to that area up there," Ed Kisch recalls. "We tried to coordinate a foot search on what I guess you could call the north side of Shunpike Road, and then we all switched over to the south side. Now, we're not talking a lot of men. We're talking two, three or four at the most."

An initial sweep of the abandoned Springfield Swim Club yielded no results. "We broke up into teams to search the quarry area because that was right by where the apartment complex was," Schwerdt recalls. Located only a short distance away from Wilson Road, the Houdaille Quarry was then—and still is today—a vast open area with its surrounding woods running adjacent to nearly the entire length of Mountview Road. The Houdaille Construction Materials Company had purchased the property from the North Jersey Quarry Company two decades prior, and the quarry had since become known for its wealth of greenockite. The quarry was also known to locals for the makeshift shooting range that the Springfield Police Department used on weekends.

The Springfield Swim Club, which had long been abandoned by the time this photo was taken in 2000. Investigators originally searched this area for clues after Jeannette's arm was recovered. The site is now the home of a large luxury apartment complex. *Photo by Mark Moran.*

Lieutenant Roy Earlman and Investigator Glenn Owens, both of the Union County Prosecutor's Office, soon arrived on the scene. The Springfield officers were split up into pairs, and the search began. Investigator Owens, described by Kisch as Union County's own "evidence guru," was there to determine whether this arm had once belonged to the victim of a potential homicide. He tailed the officers as they made their way along the unfinished dirt roadbed for Interstate 78, which ran through the quarry. Owens was determined to find any potential clues or pieces of evidence.

A short time later, Schwerdt made another gruesome discovery.

"We were over by the quarry, searching the bed that had been laid out for Interstate 78, when we found the upper portion of the arm," Schwerdt recalls. "It must have fallen off while the dog was carrying it home." Schwerdt sensed that the rest of the body must be nearby.

While Schwerdt searched what would eventually become Interstate 78, the rest of the search party made its way through thick brush and across high hills in search of the remains. Even with bright rays of sunshine peeking through the trees, these particular woods possessed an eerie atmosphere of stillness. The few sounds that could be heard were the footsteps of the search party, often accentuated by the quick swoops of the machetes that were being used to clear the masses of overgrowth and thorn bushes.

Leaving the dirt roadbed, Schwerdt and fellow patrolman Andrew Calabrese entered the Houdaille Quarry. Soon after, Schwerdt and Officer Calabrese noticed a lofty bluff overlooking the quarry floor. Determined to find the rest of the body, Schwerdt began his ascent to the top of the hill. "I had a job getting up on top of this hill," he recalls. "I had to keep pulling on shrubs and little trees to get myself up on top of this knoll. I was the first one up, and once I got to the top, I spotted the body right away."

Catching his breath, Schwerdt stood and gazed at the severely decomposed corpse lying on the ground in front of him.

"The body was lying facedown on a flat area on top of this hill," Schwerdt recalls. "I'd say that this area was maybe twenty feet around. The body was clad in a blue T-shirt and tan slacks. I immediately remembered that this was the description of the clothing that Jeannette DePalma was wearing on the day that she went missing. The body had no shoes or socks on. There were flip-flops, but they weren't on the feet; they were lying by the body. Animals had eaten most of the flesh off of her feet and all around her head."

As a patrol officer, Donald Schwerdt was no stranger to death. In the past, he had been called to the scenes of several accidents and suicides, but there was something strikingly different about this situation. Something *eerie*. What

Researcher Michael Vaccaro and author Jesse P. Pollack approaching the spot where Jeannette DePalma's remains were discovered in September 1972. *Photo by Ann Pollack.*

Schwerdt allegedly discovered arranged around this body would become a matter of controversy and intense scrutiny over the next four decades.

"There was a wooden cross over her head that was made out of two sticks. There were also some stones arranged around the top of her head in the shape of a semicircle. Almost like a halo."

As patrolman Andrew Calabrese joined him on top of the hill, Schwerdt reached for his walkie-talkie and radioed his fellow officers, letting them know that he had located the rest of the body. A horde of investigators quickly made its way up the hill, arriving within a matter of minutes. "It was just bedlam up there," Schwerdt recalls. "Everyone wanted to get up there to see what was going on." Detective Howard Thompson arrived with his camera and began thoroughly photographing the scene. Schwerdt stood still, trying not to get in Thompson's way. As the other officers and investigators began to surround him, he could not help but stare at the body, which seemed to be almost magnetically drawing the investigators closer and closer.

"I was searching the area of the Baltusrol Gardens apartments when Don Schwerdt called out over the radio that he had found a body," Ed Kisch recalls. "I drove over to Mountview Road, entered the woods, crossed a creek and went up the side of this big hill. And let me tell you, this hill was *steep*! It was a very steep angle. I can remember slipping three or four times getting up there. The body was high up on this hill. The area was a little flat at that point on the top. You could look down toward Mountview Road, which was the road that ran from Shunpike Road up to Tree Top Drive. You could look down into the quarry. The property, at that time, belonged to the Houdaille Quarry. It was an area that would not be accessible to any normal means of traffic because of where it was. In other words, no hikers or anything are really going to go there. Once I got up to the top, I saw that Don Schwerdt was still there. I believe Howard Thompson also was up there, and we were all viewing…um…what was there. It was a body—I couldn't tell you whether it was male or female, although it was *suspected* that it might have been a female because there was a pocketbook there, and the body was partially clothed. The clothing was in so-so shape, but the body was pretty deteriorated."

Schwerdt bent down to get a better look at the remains. He immediately noticed that its remaining arm was resting underneath the head, which was now little more than a skull adorned with long, dark, matted hair. He stood, contemplating the bizarre arrangement of sticks and stones that were resting around the corpse. In his mind, these items did not appear to be there by chance.

Gazing at the remains, Schwerdt's concentration was broken by a fellow officer's chilling observation.

"Don, this looks like witchcraft…"

2

THE BODY

The oldest and strongest emotion of mankind is fear, and the oldest and strongest kind of fear is fear of the unknown.
—Howard Phillips Lovecraft

While Don Schwerdt knew nothing about witchcraft, he did know that there was something very strange about the objects he saw arranged around the corpse. "It definitely was not normal to see a wooden cross and stones like that around the top of the head," he says. While Schwerdt was observing the scene around him, Ed Kisch noticed a pocketbook lying near the remains and instinctively picked it up. He opened the pocketbook and immediately began to search its contents for any trace of identification or drugs. Neither was found. Setting the pocketbook back on the ground, Kisch turned to Schwerdt and asked if he required any further assistance from him. Schwerdt shook his head, and Kisch decided to head home for the day.

By now, a swarm of police officers and investigators, all from the Springfield Police Department, the Union County Prosecutor's Office and the Union County Sheriff's Office, had begun to crowd around the body. Schwerdt was then enlisted by Detective Sergeant Sam Calabrese, brother of Patrolman Andrew Calabrese, to help keep everyone else away from the remains.

"Once the Detective Bureau came on the scene, we were pushed aside, and everything became secretive," Schwerdt remembers. "The Detective

Bureau did their own thing, and it wasn't discussed with us. They treated the rest of us patrolmen like a bunch of dunces."

While Schwerdt began ordering the other responding officers away from the body, the detectives discussed what the appropriate next step would be. They decided that trying to carry the corpse out of the wilderness would be too risky. The cliff where the body was lying was surrounded on three sides by treacherous slopes littered with overgrown thorn bushes, and the fourth side was a steep, forty-foot drop to the quarry floor below. The investigators eventually decided to lower the remains to the quarry floor by means of an aerial truck ladder.

"That was the easiest way to take that body out of there," Ed Kisch recalls. "The side of that hill was just too steep, so we called the fire department and had them use their ladder truck to remove the body from the quarry side." Springfield's fire chief, Robert Day, was radioed and asked to stand by while the detectives awaited the arrival of Union County's chief medical examiner, Dr. Bernard Ehrenberg. It would be Ehrenberg's job to perform the formality of officially declaring the partially skeletonized remains as dead.

Abandoned equipment litters the floor of the Houdaille Quarry. The Devil's Teeth cliff can be seen in the background. *Photo by Mark Moran.*

Ed Cardinal, a seven-year veteran of the Springfield Volunteer Fire Department, was on a SCUBA training assignment in Ledgewood when he became aware that his fellow firefighters were standing by to help recover a body that had been found on top of a wooded cliff in the Houdaille Quarry. Cardinal knew the cliff well.

"*The Devil's Teeth*. That's what it was called back then," Cardinal remembers. "It was originally known as the Devil's Skull back in the 1920s. When my dad was a kid, he told me about an old dirt road that extended from Summit, over the hill where Shunpike Road crosses what is now Route 78, then south, passing the east side of the mountain where the body was found and then down toward Trenton.

"Somewhere on the side of the mountain lived a man by the name of Andrew Jackson. He was known for bringing bog iron up from South Jersey and smelting barbells, sash weights and other items along that trail. As a kid, my father and his friends would walk that trail, looking for old barbell plates and dumbbells, which had been poorly cast and discarded.

"While traversing that mountaintop, my father and his friends found a natural depression in the bluestone where the overburden of soil had been blown or washed away. That rock hollow would fill with rainwater and become a natural birdbath. He told me about how kids would scoop the dirt and mud out of the depression, and subsequent rainstorms would keep the water fresh. This allowed them to sit around in the water like a hot tub, but eventually, the bird crap and mud would turn the water foul.

"In the autumn months, the spot became a dreary place. More often than not, turkey buzzards could be seen circling the spot, looking for drowned mice and other creatures, and the bowl of the rock depression would dry out, taking on the appearance of the inside of an inverted half skull. That's how the place came to be known as the Devil's Skull.

"That spot was always a strange and a dismal place," Cardinal continues. "Even when they built the apartments nearby on Wilson Road, people said, 'Who would want to live there?' And this was long before Route 78 was cleared. There was an abandoned pool and swim club right behind those apartments as well. A really dismal, spooky place. It later became the town's leaf dump.

"Decades later, when the Houdaille Construction Materials Company started mining the area, the steam shovels with clamshell buckets would dump their loads of overburden and waste rock along the edge of the Devil's Skull. Back then, there weren't very many trees there, so when the small piles of waste were lined up in a row, they looked just like teeth

The Devil's Teeth cliff in Springfield's Houdaille Quarry. Jeannette DePalma's remains were found on top of this cliff on September 19, 1972. *Photo by Mark Moran.*

along a jaw. The Devil's Skull now became the Devil's Teeth, and that's where they found the body."

While the investigators awaited the arrival of Dr. Ehrenberg, members of Springfield's Detective Bureau began combing the area around the body for any trace evidence. After hours of searching the scene, it became apparent that no pieces of evidence that might lead to an obvious cause of death would be found. "The best that I can recall," Kisch says, "there was nothing that was found there that could be used to conclusively say that foul play was suspected in any way, shape or form." This was not only a cause of frustration for the group of investigators but also a cause for legitimate concern. If there was no evidence to suggest that this was a homicide, suicide or accident, how then, the investigators wondered, did this body come to rest in this desolate area?

One person who was especially troubled by this was Don Schwerdt. "As a parent, this stood out to me," he says, looking back. Standing over the decomposing remains of what he believed to be a missing teenage girl, Don thought to himself, "This could have been one of my kids…"

At 6:05 p.m., a little over two hours after the discovery of the remains, Dr. Bernard Ehrenberg arrived on the hill and officially pronounced the body dead. "It was a more of a formality," Kisch remarks. "It was obvious to anyone with a set of eyes that the girl was dead, but we couldn't proceed until an official declaration was made by Ehrenberg, and even that, at most, was just him walking up to the body, pointing at it and saying, 'Yup, she's dead. Take her away.' That's all."

The fire department was radioed and told to proceed to the quarry, and a short time later, Springfield's American LaFrance ladder truck arrived. The truck was backed up against the cliff's rocky wall, and the eighty-five-foot aerial ladder was raised about halfway to the cliff's edge. Fireman Don Stewart ascended the ladder and joined the detectives at the scene. Stewart, a Vietnam veteran, was visibly shaken at the sight of the body.

"Don Stewart was an easygoing, fun-loving guy before Vietnam," Cardinal recalls. "After he returned from 'Nam and was hired on to the fire department, his demeanor changed. Even though he acted upbeat in public, in private he seemed sad all the time. Don was the spitting image of Woody Harrelson and probably spent as much time in a real bar as Woody did acting in one on *Cheers*. Helping bring Jeannette down from the mountain bothered Don greatly, and he talked about it often in the days and weeks following the whole event. He told me that her body was grayish brown, like leather. I remember him saying that her body didn't look like the body of a person that had been beat up or killed in an accident. Those types would be sprawled out or distorted or in a kind of fetal position. He said that she looked peaceful—almost like she was sleeping—and that really bothered him."

Only one year after assisting with the recovery of Jeannette's body, Don Stewart would commit suicide by shooting himself in the heart. He was surrounded by fellow Springfield firefighters and police officers, all begging him to drop his pistol. "In addition to some other things, I do believe that the DePalma incident weighed heavily on him," Cardinal says in retrospect. "Don was always in turmoil after Vietnam. Important things became minor, and minor things became important to him. Girls were a bad issue, as was drinking. Another member of the department, Ted Johnson, was always at odds with Don. Ted was higher up on the totem pole. The two of them always seemed to rub one another the wrong way. For no real reason, Ted would sneak around and try to catch Don and many others committing minor infractions. This guy was really high-strung, and he really annoyed Don, to say the least. Well, underneath it all, Ted had problems of his own and eventually threatened to take his life. One day, he just locked himself in his basement, and his wife heard a gunshot. It got real quiet, and when he didn't answer her calling for him, she went ballistic. When the police arrived and broke into the basement, they found him just sitting on the floor with a bullet hole in the wall. Turns out, this guy had no intention of shooting himself. Ted told the cops that he just wanted to scare his wife. Well, he was sent off to a 'special place' for a few years, and when he came back, the department *promoted* the guy! Don Stewart made Ted Johnson into the laughing stock of the whole department. I don't remember the exact words he used, but things like 'ditzeldork' and 'wiener' were usually followed by references to Ted's aiming ability and so on. It was intense!"

Ed Cardinal believes that Stewart's taunting of Johnson would later backfire on the young firefighter and contribute to his own eventual suicide.

"Sometime later, Don hooked up with a rather high-end female, and one night, he showed up outside her apartment with a gun. I honestly don't remember what exactly set him off. It may have been another guy showing up at her apartment, or she could have just dumped him or whatever. Someone called the Springfield Police Department, and they called our fire chief, Ed Erskine, and asked him to go calm Don down. Once Deputy Chief Erskine showed up, Don became convinced that he was about to lose his job. On top of that, after all this time, Don had been belittling Ted for 'not having the guts' to shoot himself, and now he was in *the exact same spot*. I think, in Don's mind, there was no turning back at that point, especially with everyone watching. It was just a total shock to everyone. Don and I were good friends. Chief Erskine was real shook up over it. He told us all that he believed that if everyone had just [gone] away, Don would have just put the gun down and [gone] home."

With his suicide, Don Stewart became the first victim of the so-called DePalma Curse, which allegedly befell the Springfield Fire Department after Jeannette's body was recovered. According to Ed Cardinal, Chief Robert Day quit the department and went to work as a janitor in a local school. Deputy Chief Ed Erskine gave up "years of conservative thinking," quit the fire department, divorced his wife and ended up living in his car for several years. Another fellow firefighter needed to take a leave of absence for "mental rehabilitation," while yet another randomly quit the department without giving any reason.

While Cardinal acknowledges the veracity of these claims, he refuses to believe in any kind of DePalma Curse. Looking back, Cardinal says, "I seriously doubt that the DePalma incident had any bearing on the fates of the majority of these men. It was just a sad, unfortunate day for the department. Whatever happened to those guys afterward was just a 'bad luck happens' kind of thing…"

Ed Cardinal in 1968. After retiring from the Springfield Fire
Department, Cardinal began writing articles for *Weird NJ* magazine
and was instrumental in assisting the authors with their research for this
book. *Photo by Don Stewart.*

Back at the quarry, a body bag was retrieved, and the detectives carefully
placed the remains inside. "They wanted to do everything they could to preserve
the integrity of the body," Don Schwerdt recalls. The bag was then bundled
up and placed onto a Stokes stretcher. The Springfield Fire Department had
decided to remove Jeannette's remains by means of a method that was usually
reserved for incapacitated victims of a disaster or serious accident.

"Back then, the standard operating procedure was to tie a rope to a rung
at the base of the ladder, lay the rope on all of the rungs, then drop the
rope over the top rung and let it fall to the ground with a lot of slack," Ed
Cardinal explains. "You would then secure the rope to the stretcher. All the
while, the ladder and two ladder extensions would remain in the truck's bed.

Then, as you lifted the ladder, the stretcher would rise to a predetermined height when the slack was taken up. As you extended the extension ladders, the stretcher would rise the rest of the way at half the speed that the ladder was extending, as the balance of the slack was used up. Reverse would lower the stretcher at half speed, be gentler and would be easier to control. Sometimes, tormentor ropes would be tied to stretchers in order to keep them from spinning or to guide them away from trees or wires."

Once the body had been lowered to the quarry floor, the multitude of detectives, patrolmen, firefighters and county investigators all made their way down from the cliff using the same aerial ladder. "I remember the guys at the bottom of the cliff shaking the ladder to rile up Calabrese," Schwerdt recalls with a laugh. "Sam was afraid of heights, you see."

The body was then loaded into the back of an ambulance and driven to the Sullivan Funeral Home in nearby Roselle. "We were using Sullivan's morgue back in those days," Schwerdt remembers. "It had better facilities than ours." Once the body arrived, Dr. Ehrenberg began a preliminary examination of the remains, which yielded no apparent cause of death.

Ed Kisch was not surprised by Dr. Ehrenberg's failure to determine what had killed Jeannette. "Bernie Ehrenberg was *not* a trained pathologist," Kisch recalls. "The guy was a friggin' physician! You know how Bernie Ehrenberg got his job? *Political appointment.* Bernie Ehrenberg was not competent enough, as far as I am concerned, to have been conducting forensic autopsies. I know for a fact that he botched the autopsy of another high-profile murder victim that was found up on Springfield Top." When asked if he was referring to the 1976 murder of Springfield resident Beverly Manoff, Kisch laughs. "We'll let that one lie," he says. "I can tell you this, though: that murder will *never* be solved."

Back at the morgue, Dr. Ehrenberg eventually decided to have the body X-rayed for any possible bone fractures, bullet holes or knife strikes. The remains were carefully wrapped up and driven to Elizabeth General Hospital, about three miles from the funeral home. "Forensic science was in its infancy in 1972. If you wanted to X-ray a body, you had to drive to Elizabeth," Schwerdt recalls.

The X-rays revealed no bone breaks or fractures. Further adding to the frustration of the investigators, no bullet holes or knife strikes were found either. The investigators decided to focus their efforts on identifying the remains while Ehrenberg ordered further tests. Calabrese remembered Detective Olivo's statement regarding the supposed local runaway Jeannette DePalma and decided to start there. Due to the extensive decomposition of the remains, Calabrese figured he would likely need dental records for a positive identification. The office of Jeannette's dentist would be the detective sergeant's first stop.

This particular dentist agreed to speak with us, but only if his demands of anonymity were met. Cleary agitated and anxious, the dentist feared any kind of possible repercussions for his comments regarding Jeannette and his involvement with the investigation into her death.

"I am glad to give you any information that I remember, but I don't want my name associated with this," the dentist says. "Jeannette was not your all-American girl, if you know what I mean. She was odd. She hung around with a rough crowd. The kind of kids you wouldn't want your own children around. I'd definitely say she was a troubled kid. This family was a peculiar family, and I don't know what you know about them. At the time, it was a very harrowing experience. These people still live around here. I'm frightened of these people, quite frankly, and I don't want them showing up at my door. I have my own feelings about who this family is, and I don't want to go into it. The bottom line is, they were *odd*, to say the least. An odd family. They are still in this neighborhood, and I don't want to be part of why they are angry because, quite frankly, I will have bad nights thinking about these people, um…looking to get me because I identified their daughter. I mean, they were strange people. I just want you to know that. Do you understand the circumstances? This was an unsolved ritual murder or whatever it was, and I am still close to this neighborhood and they were strange people. They were a big family. I don't want somebody knocking on my door, saying, 'You touched my daughter!' You follow what I'm saying? This is not a happy thing for me. It is something that has haunted this area for a long time."

Jeannette's dentist then began to recount the day that he was asked to assist in the identification of her body. "I was fresh out of dental school around this time," he says. "My father, who[m] I shared the practice with, got all of the older patients, and I got all the kids. Jeannette was one of them. One day, at about three thirty in the afternoon, this detective named Calabrese walked into my office. He goes, 'I need you to come with me,' and I laughed at him. I said, 'What am I, under arrest or something?' And he told me, 'No, we have a body to identify.' I told him that I currently had patients and to come back at five thirty, after I had closed up."

If the dentist's recollections are accurate, his encounter with Calabrese most likely occurred the day after Jeannette's body was located, as the detective sergeant was still searching for her remains at 3:30 p.m. the previous day.

"I knew these guys, and I knew it wasn't a joke," the dentist recalls. "I'd seen Calabrese around before. He sometimes worked as a crossing guard at one of the schools." When Calabrese returned, he instructed the young dentist to bring along Jeannette DePalma's dental records. "I knew that she was missing," he says. "Everyone in town said that she was a runaway." Calabrese then drove him to the Sullivan Funeral Home, where Ehrenberg was waiting with the remains.

When the dentist arrived, he was taken straight to the morgue. "The body was on a metal morgue table, and that table was covered in plastic," he says. "When I arrived, they kind of unfolded the plastic so that I could have access to the body. There was really no identifiable body to speak of. It was all dried up. You couldn't even tell if the body was male or female. The clothes were more identifiable than the body. I could tell that she had been wearing a T-shirt and jeans. The clothes were all beat up and dried up. The bones still had flesh in some areas, but it was all shriveled. It reminded me of the cadavers that we used in dental school. Calabrese then handed me Jeannette's skull. The skull and mandible were intact, and the skull still had hair on it." The dentist then began to compare Jeannette DePalma's dental records to the recovered mandible, tooth by tooth. "Her X-rays were recent. I had put fillings in earlier that summer." After careful examination, the dentist confirmed that the mandible belonged to Jeannette DePalma. "I was able to determine from the dental records that it was her," he recalls. "I'll never forget that day. I had never been asked to identify a body before…"

Now armed with a positive identification, Detective Sergeant Sam Calabrese could finally notify the DePalma family and make an official statement to the press.

At some point during Dr. Ehrenberg's subsequent round of tests, the determination was made that, while no official cause of death could be determined, it was possible that Jeannette DePalma had been the victim of strangulation. This determination was eventually leaked to the press, and in the minds of countless Springfield residents, Jeannette DePalma was now officially being considered the victim of a homicide. Ed Kisch, however, had his doubts. "Ehrenberg never came up with a specific cause of death. There were some innuendos that were made by him, but I won't go into those because innuendoes are not worth anything when it comes to police work. They're rumors, as far as any of that is concerned. Ehrenberg could not positively determine that she was strangled. He could not positively determine whether or not she had been beaten with some type of instrument. There was no indication from him, from what I was able to understand, that there were any damages to the bones. There was no indication that she was shot. Those were things that, I believe, were not able to be proven by the pathological examination, so what we had was a suspicious death because of where the body was ultimately located."

In addition to the perceived evidence of strangulation, Ehrenberg made another rather curious discovery. In 2004, *Weird NJ* magazine reported that after Jeannette's autopsy, "a tissue sample submitted for toxicological examination proved unsuitable for alcohol analysis, but determined that there was a lead content in the body of .694 mg." The source of this information has since been lost to time, but it has been confirmed by the DePalma family. "My uncle Frank knew a guy at the medical examiner's office," recalls Racheal Sajeski, the daughter of Jeannette's older sister Gwendolyn. "He went down there in the 1980s to ask about the lead content and was told to back down. They told him to stop asking questions and to leave it alone."

John Bancey, the son of Jeannette's older sister Darlene, told a similar story during a 2004 interview with *Weird NJ* magazine. "My uncle Frank, that's [Jeannette's] brother, he had a friend in the medical examiner's office, and he said that something wasn't right. My uncle pushed the issue and pushed the issue, and he started to get threatened, told he would be arrested if he didn't stop. Because he was questioning everybody. He was pretty upset about it."

A blood lead concentration of 0.694mg/L is a significantly high level for a teenager. Slightly higher levels have been known to lead to permanent brain damage and death. The symptoms of lead poisoning include weight loss, insomnia, anemia, abdominal pain, memory loss and a tingling sensation felt in the body's extremities. Jeannette DePalma, however, seemed to exhibit none of these symptoms around the time she died. Jeannette's mother, Florence, told the *Elizabeth Daily Journal* that her daughter "had a slight cold" on the day she vanished, but no other ailments were mentioned. It is also safe to assume that a teenager suffering from a fatal bout of lead poisoning would not feel well enough to run away from home.

With this in mind, the matter of how such a high amount of lead entered Jeannette's body is shrouded in mystery. Dr. Randall C. Baselt's *Disposition of Toxic Drugs and Chemicals in Man* cites a study in which the children of "industrially-exposed fathers" were found to have blood lead concentrations from 0.30mg/L to 0.80mg/L. This occurrence was due to lead dust being carried home on the clothing of parents working in the industrial field. Is it possible that Jeannette's father, an automotive wrecker, brought lead dust into his home?

If that were the case, the professional opinions of those who believe Jeannette's exposure to lead was antemortem would be significantly bolstered. "I am not aware of lead being formed postmortem in a decomposing body," says Dr. Cyril Wecht, one of the world's leading forensic pathologists.

Dr. Judy Melinek, however, believes that there might be an alternative explanation. Dr. Melinek, a forensic pathologist who worked to identify victims of the September 11, 2001 terrorist attacks, theorizes that the ground on which Jeannette was lying might hold the key. "The biggest problem is the lead in our soil," Dr. Melinek says. "One question would be how much soil was in the sample taken from the victim." In her professional opinion, a contaminated tissue sample could have led to these test results. "During the 1970s, a lot of lead got into soil from lead paint because it was only banned in 1978," Dr. Melinek continues. "This may be a real level and background for contaminated soil in the '70s."

After the inconclusive autopsy, the dried and decaying clothing of Jeannette DePalma was packed up, along with her pocketbook, and returned to the Springfield Police Department. Once the clothing and pocketbook made their way back to the police station, the bizarre and arguably unprofessional decision was made to have Jeannette DePalma's clothing hung over a large air conditioning unit on the side of the building. "They had the clothes hanging there for a good three, four days or better," Schwerdt remembers. "I don't know why they had them hanging there."

"There weren't a whole lot of brain surgeons on the job in those days," retired Springfield lieutenant Peter Hammer says with a laugh. "You were lucky if half of us could read or write back then."

"It was just like a clothesline with her shirt and her slacks hanging on it," Don Schwerdt recalls. "They stunk the whole department up. It was awful. Once you see death, you don't forget the smell."

Ed Kisch remembers the clothing and pocketbook eventually being boxed up and sent to the New Jersey State Police's crime lab for further forensic testing. "Normally, if you were to send clothing evidence to the state police or the FBI, they would want you to dry the clothing out," he says. "There were maggots crawling all over Jeannette's clothing. That was from the flesh. After awhile, it stunk. I can remember some of the officers started to scream and yell about the clothes being out there. Chief Parsell got on that bandwagon and yelled at Sam Calabrese. 'Get those clothes out of there! They don't belong out there!' he said. Finally, they were moved and sent out. I never did find out if they got anything off of the clothing or the purse. By that point, the Detective Bureau was handling the case, and they weren't very talkative."

Don Schwerdt shares the same sentiment. "The case was not discussed with the patrol division at all. It was like it was all over. The Detective Bureau was very hush-hush back in those days, and once they handled it, the patrol division was cut out. They didn't give us any information after that. It was all very tightlipped. They wouldn't give us guys in the patrol division the time of day. They used to call us 'F Troop.'" The Detective Bureau's nickname for patrolmen such as Don Schwerdt and Ed Kisch was a rather unflattering reference to the ABC sitcom *F Troop*, which aired from 1965 until 1967. The series, starring Forrest Tucker, often employed slapstick humor and showcased the exploits of a group of inept United States soldiers in the late 1860s.

Back at the Springfield police station, rumors began to run rampant regarding an incident that had occurred, allegedly involving Jeannette's detached arm.

The wife of a retired Springfield police officer who has asked not to be identified recalls being told that after Jeannette's arm was found on Wilson Road, it was brought back to the Springfield police station and placed in the break room refrigerator. "After that, while everyone else was out in the quarry looking for the rest of the girl, some of the other officers thought it would be funny to put the arm on top of another policeman's lunch to scare him," she recalls with disgust.

"That rumor is the perfect example of how things tended to snowball out of proportion with this case," Kisch says. "The arm was placed in the refrigerator in an effort to preserve it as a whole in case further testing was necessary. Why this particular fridge? It was the only one in the police department that could hold the arm, and it had limited access. The only other place would have been a morgue, and at that time, the department was using local funeral homes for autopsies. The arm's chain of custody was no longer so important, as it actually had been removed from the crime scene by a dog and therefore had already been contaminated. We could not sign off on the chain of custody form because that chain had been broken by the dog. I can't even answer if Ehrenberg ever conclusively said that the arm was or wasn't Jeannette's. It was *assumed* that after the rest of the body was located, and that there was an arm missing from it, that the arm in evidence and the body belonged to each other. Anyway, as far as any prank goes, that's all bullshit. Del Tompkins, who was the juvenile officer at the time, took his lunch out of the fridge and sat down to eat it. The other guys in the break room said, 'Whoa! Are you really gonna eat that, Del? It was in there with a friggin' arm, for Chrissakes!' And Del said, 'I don't give a shit what it was in there with, I'm hungry!' So that's where that story came from. No prank, just a bunch of guys busting Del's chops."

This would not be the last rumor to surface regarding the strange case of Jeannette DePalma, the supposed "runaway" about whom everyone in Springfield had heard and read yet no one seemed to truly know.

3

THE "RUNAWAY"

I had the story, bit by bit, from various people, and, as generally happens in such cases, each time it was a different story.
—*Edith Wharton,* Ethan Frome

The young woman who would come to be known as "the girl on the mountain" was born Jeannette Christine DePalma on August 3, 1956, in Jersey City, New Jersey, to Florence, a homemaker, and Salvatore DePalma, the owner and operator of D&D Auto Salvage in Newark. Jeannette was the sixth child born to a large Italian Catholic family, which would grow to a total of seven children with the birth of her sister Cynthia the following year. The DePalma family resided in Roselle before relocating to the township of Springfield in the mid-1960s, purchasing the large house at 4 Clearview Drive for $65,000. Today, the property is valued at more than $500,000. For the DePalmas, suburban Springfield seemed like the ideal place to settle down and raise their large family.

Located in the heart of Union County, the township of Springfield was formed in the late eighteenth century, with its roots heavily planted in the American Revolution. It was during the Battle of Springfield that the iconic command of "Give 'em Watts, boys!" was bellowed by the Reverend James Caldwell. Caldwell, a Continental army chaplain, provided his soldiers with stacks of hymnals that had been published by Isaac Watts, an English theologian, to use as wadding for their guns.

A young Jeannette DePalma (center) pictured alongside her sisters Cindy and Gwendolyn. *Courtesy of the DePalma family.*

Several decades later, vast changes would take place that eventually transformed Springfield from the small farm town that it was into the upper-middle-class community it is today. In the 1920s, a large swamp near the geographical center of town was used as a depository for ammunition, chemicals and other leftovers from the First World War. The swamp was deemed an optimal place, as these harmful items would be out of sight from residents and nearly inaccessible, except by steam-powered railroad. This, however, did not stop the local curious youth from eventually finding their way to the depository. Those same children would eventually grow up and fight in the next world war, passing tales of the swamp's orange water, rust-colored dirt and bubbling ground to the next generation.

During the Great Depression, the United States government formed what were known as CCC (Civilian Conservation Corps) camps. Able-bodied men were put to work removing the leftover World War I ammunition from the swamp. The area was filled in, and a large athletic field was built on top. The older residents of Springfield began to express deep concern about the harsh chemicals and ammunition byproducts that lay buried beneath an athletic field—a field that seemed to produce only the greenest of grass. However, the townspeople's concerns fell on deaf ears, and the athletic field sat untouched for years before Springfield finally decided to clean up the area.

By the early 1940s, Springfield had become the quintessential all-American town. The town's center—which, ironically, was not positioned in the center of town—contained every pleasantry and necessity that a resident of Springfield could reasonably need. There was a hardware store, a butcher's shop, a bakery and a malt shop, as well as the local barber, doctor and dentist. All were easily accessible via a trolley track running down the center of Morris Avenue. A large automobile repair shop was located on the far end of town, while the east end boasted an old-fashioned automobile dealer, as well as a lumberyard and the centuries-old First Presbyterian Church of Springfield. The church still casts a large shadow over Morris Avenue to this very day. Around the corner from this church is a Revolutionary War–era cemetery, along with the historic "Cannonball House," which now houses the Springfield Historical Society. The house got its peculiar moniker after a British cannonball pierced its walls during the Battle of Springfield. The Cannonball House was one of only four homes left standing after the British retreat. The historical society continues to display the famed cannonball, and over the years that followed, several hundred more would continue to be found in the nearby Rahway River.

As the years went on, Springfield's old wooden firehouse was moved to a new brick building, and the municipal building was constructed to look like all of the other new brick buildings that were popping up all over the Garden State. Brand-new houses began to appear on the side roads off Morris Avenue. The new homes, with their bright white façades and evergreen shutters, all seemed to resemble the popular Sears & Roebuck "Modern Home." These predesigned houses gained prominence in the post–World War II American suburbs.

In the early 1950s, the farmers on the south end of town were selling off their land, and new developments of rather small houses on five-thousand-square-foot lots were built. By 1960, the development houses had begun to grow in size, and almost all took the shape of the popular split-level homes that were being constructed on quarter-acre lots. During this time, an ethnic change was beginning to take place in Springfield. As more and more developments were built on old farmland, the once-familiar social roles played by the north and south sides of town were now being reversed. The south side of Springfield began to fill up with families moving in from the larger cities of Manhattan and Long Island. A large portion of those families were either Italian or, in most cases, Jewish. "While there never seemed to be a seething animosity toward any ethnic group in Springfield," Ed Cardinal recalls, "there now was a slight edge between the tightknit farming families that had once held prominence in town and the new 'city slickers.' The edge between the two groups rarely, if ever, warranted a fight or argument, but both sides eventually began to gravitate toward their own respective cliques. The children of the town's farmers had the Future Farmers of America organization and farming courses at school. The Presbyterians, or 'preppies,' had their school functions and varsity sports. Finally, the 'city slickers' had their parties and dances. Despite these differences, the younger residents of Springfield all seemed to get along with each other, for the most part."

This, unfortunately, would not be the case with some of the older townspeople. In one particular instance, a gentleman from New York City who served on Springfield's town council told a popular New York City newspaper that Springfield was "a fine up-and-coming Jewish community." This statement would prove to be controversial to some of Springfield's gentile residents. "From that point on, the town council seemed to seesaw back and forth between Italian, Jewish and 'old-time' politicians," Ed Cardinal continues. "For years, the town council never seemed to get things right. The fire department suffered, the police department suffered, all while realtors and lawyers bickered back and forth. People argued that the newcomers were building too many baseball fields. They complained about the newcomers wanting fancy things like sidewalks, paid fire departments and better streets. They complained that the old-timers only hired cops, firemen and town workers from the old-time families and that the newcomers only hired the lawyers from their own ranks. The bickering and lawsuits never seemed to end. It was all very 'us against them,' but nobody could really define who *us* or *them* really were."

On the positive side, Springfield was beginning to garner a respectable reputation for its clean streets and parks, along with its lack of graffiti, litter or run-down areas. Springfield's churchgoing citizens ensured that no "negative" establishments such as adult bookstores, biker bars or tattoo parlors would be allowed in town. Car washes and pinball machines were not permitted, and ordinances were passed that prevented cars on blocks, recreational vehicles or boats being housed in front yards. The residents of Springfield could also proudly boast of the township's lack of gang activity or violence. "There were no gangs to speak of, but there were a few interesting characters in town," Ed Cardinal says with a laugh. "There was Tilly, an extremely short and fat one-eyed woman with one huge breast. There was the lady who swept 'moonbeams' off of her driveway all night long, as well as the mailman who ended up living in a dumpster in Las Vegas. And then there was 'Faaah.' 'Faaah' would walk down the streets of Springfield late at night, slamming street sign after street sign with his palm, shouting '*FAAAH!*' over and over again." Cardinal can recall even more colorful residents of Springfield. "There was the Mechanical Man, a guy that walked just like a robot all the time. Another guy would wander around town claiming to be a visitor from Mars, as well as an FBI agent. And finally, there was Tony. Tony was a little short guy in a hard hat who would stand on the side of the road with a clipboard, counting every single car that passed by him. And then there were the rest of us…"

In the mid-1960s, construction began on a series of large houses on the mountaintop located on Springfield's west side. A new street, Mountview Road, was cut across the mountain with the sole purpose of servicing these new homes. For many years to come, Mountview Road would be known as "the new road" to the longtime residents of Springfield. The creation of this brand-new neighborhood, dubbed "Springfield Top," meant that the fire department would need larger and faster trucks and that the police department would need more officers and more patrol vehicles. The residents of Springfield who were not fortunate enough to live in this new and affluent area soon complained about having to pay for services that benefitted only the new residents. With their purchase of 4 Clearview Drive, the DePalma family instantly became one of the many new mountaintop residents for whom the original townsfolk held a special level of disdain.

As if this were not enough, further attention was drawn to the DePalmas due to what many perceived as strange behavior. Several Springfield residents recall the family rarely leaving their home, and when they did, they seldom spoke with neighbors. In a close-knit community like Springfield, families that kept to themselves could expect to have suspicious eyes laid on them. "Something wasn't 100 percent with that family," recalls a former acquaintance of the DePalmas. "They were weird."

Ed Kisch remembers being called to the DePalma residence several times in the early 1970s. "Sal and Florence would get into a fight, someone would call us and, by the time we got there, Florence would turn us away. She'd say things like, 'Well, there *was* a problem, but now there's not.' We were constantly getting called up to that house on Clearview Drive."

The former DePalma home at 4 Clearview Drive in Springfield. *Photo by Jesse P. Pollack.*

Racheal Sajeski confirms Kisch's account of these events. "My grandpa Sal was rotten to my grandmother," she recalls.

Once she grew into adolescence, Jeannette, the second-youngest daughter of the DePalma family, found herself the focus of local gossip. Margaret Bandrowski, now a Springfield Township committeewoman, taught at Union Catholic Regional High School in the 1970s when Jeannette was a student. Bandrowski can recall being privy to the hearsay surrounding the young pupil. "I knew who she was, but I did not *know* her," she says. "Judging by what I heard from other students, Jeannette was a little on the wild side. Now, I don't exactly know the specifics of what 'wild' necessarily meant for her, but in those days, it usually connoted that she hung around with boys, maybe did some drugs or smoked. Stuff like that." Bandrowski admits that these connotations seem pretty tame by today's standards. "You must remember that this was a different era," she muses. "I don't think 'wild' meant anything other than that Jeannette was not the perfect Christian child that her mother believed her to be. I have no reason to think the girl did anything more than experiment with drugs of some kind, and that may not have gone much beyond anything other kids were doing at that time."

Roy Simpson, a former resident of nearby Mountainside, remembers being privy to neighborhood rumors regarding Jeannette's alleged "wild" behavior when he was a child. "She was supposedly promiscuous," he says. "That was the talk at the time. We didn't really hear too much about drugs. Mind you, I was only about eleven at the time, but we would mostly hear of the sisters' promiscuity."

"Back at the station, we used to call Jeannette 'Party Girl,'" Kisch recalls. "I can recall quite a few instances where I had to pull that kid out of the backseat of some guy's car over at Briant Park." Located only one mile away from the Houdaille Quarry, Springfield's Briant Park was a popular lovers' lane in the early 1970s.

Gail Donohue, Jeannette's closest friend, casts doubt on Kisch's recollections of encountering Jeannette at Briant Park. "I don't think that was Jeannette at all," she says. "I mean, she and I both had crushes on these two Italian guys in Berkeley Heights, but I wasn't even allowed

Jeannette DePalma as a student at Union Catholic Regional High School in 1970. *Courtesy of Union Catholic Regional High School.*

to date until I was sixteen. We would all meet up during the day in the summertime, and again, I knew she liked this one guy. They would make out in his car or whatever, but I think that was in Berkeley Heights, not Briant Park. I think that cop is off in thinking that was Jeannette…"

Cindy DePalma is far more direct in her assessment of Kisch's memory. "This cop seems to be feeding people a lot of bullshit," she says.

Kisch's recollection is also somewhat contradicted by a statement that then detective sergeant Sam Calabrese gave to the *Elizabeth Daily Journal.*

The Wednesday, September 20, 1972 edition featured an article entitled "Find Body Atop Cliff," in which Calabrese claimed that Jeannette "had no record of trouble with the authorities" and described her as "an attractive girl, about five feet, four inches in height."

When we asked Ed Kisch to explain this apparent discrepancy between his own personal recollections regarding Jeannette's alleged disreputable activities and Calabrese's statements to the media, Kisch replied, "Look, she may not have had any *formal* complaints signed against her, but she was far from a good kid. Del Tompkins had been up to that house several times in reference to her. I don't believe that there had been serious juvenile matters, but I do believe there was a reference card on her in Del's office. Del knew all the kids in town. If you wanted to ask about a kid, there wasn't anything that he couldn't tell you."

Don Schwerdt, however, does not recall Jeannette ever having any interaction with the Springfield Police Department. "As far as I know, nobody had any recollection of Jeannette being involved with any police activity, or being picked up or questioned for anything," he says. When asked if he was aware that Jeannette had been referred to as "Party Girl" by other members of the police force, Schwerdt bewilderedly says, "That's the first I've heard of that!"

When asked if Jeannette had any kind of arrest record for delinquency or narcotics possession, Ed Kisch replied, "There is a possibility there, but even if I knew, I wouldn't tell you. I would not reveal that information to you because you're not entitled to it. To be honest with you, when I took over the Juvenile Bureau, I never specifically looked at her card index file. Del did have one, but it took me a specific period of time to get everything straightened out and put in order. He did a good job as a juvenile officer. I did look at some of the cases that he worked on. Records were the only thing that kept you and the juvenile officer in power. Del was born and raised in the town, and so was I, so there wasn't anything with any of the kids or any of the people that I didn't know. I knew a lot of people in that town. So I will tell you, as a patrol officer, I could find her in the backseat of cars and that they had been partying."

Melissa Benner, a longtime friend of Jeannette's, acknowledges that some of the rumors regarding her friend were not without merit. "All teens did things like hitchhike and smoke pot back then," she says, implying that Jeannette was no exception. "She and I met in the late 1960s at Our Lady of Lourdes Catholic School in Mountainside. We played kickball, snuck cigarettes and visited each other's homes. She was a good person. Just a normal teenager."

Jeannette's cousin Lisa Treich Greulich recalls spending a large amount of time with the "normal teenager" in the final years leading up to her death. "We were hippie Jesus freaks who smoked weed," she laughs. "We used to smoke and listen to rock music. Janis Joplin was her favorite. She really loved Janis." While acknowledging her cousin's recreational drug use, Lisa is also quick to point out that much of the rumors regarding Jeannette have been exaggerated over the years. "Jeannette *did* smoke pot, but it was only occasionally, and it was only if someone else had some and offered it to her. She certainly didn't go around looking to buy it or anything. Jeannette didn't even drink!"

When asked if Jeannette engaged in any kind of hard drug use—the kind that could have killed her with an overdose—Gail Donohue laughs. "I can't imagine that at all," she says. "My father was an executive, but he came from a very poor background. His father died after falling off of a construction building in Atlanta while my grandmother was pregnant with him during the Great Depression. My father and his cousins were all brought up together. So my father became a self-made man, and he became very appreciative of his compliments. We always had fine china. He always had a very impressive liquor cabinet. He always had every cognac—everything a man could want. One time, Jeannette and I snuck a sip of schnapps and maybe a little whiskey from my father's liquor cabinet. She then suggested that we jump up and down to 'mix it up.' She said, 'Maybe we'll get drunk quicker.' So, if you're asking whether or not Jeannette had knowledge of hardcore drug use, my answer is no. *Hell* no."

Public controversy regarding Jeannette DePalma's supposed drug use erupted when Florence DePalma was quoted in the *Elizabeth Daily Journal* as saying her daughter had used "nothing serious like heroin" but had been under the influence of "pills" and "maybe marijuana." The *Daily Journal* further quoted Mrs. DePalma as saying, "Once Jeannette received Jesus, she stopped using drugs." This matter was further complicated when the very next issue of the *Elizabeth Daily Journal* hit newsstands featuring a follow-up article in which Florence DePalma denied ever saying that Jeannette had used drugs. Florence was quoted in this new article as saying, "Jeannette was not a drug user, and by her witness of Jesus and with Jesus' help had turned children from drugs." The source of this apparent confusion was never made clear by either party.

Today, Lisa Treich Greulich remembers many nights spent with her rebellious cousins, in which the three would hitch rides from strangers. "Jeannette, Cindy and I used to run away from home and hitchhike to

Elizabeth so that we could see these three boys: Joe, John and 'Nubs.' Nubs's real name was Wayne, but we called him 'Nubs' because he was missing his thumbs. Cindy went out with Nubs, I went out with Joe and Jeannette went out with John." Lisa does not recall the last names of these three young men.

"I can remember one night in particular where Jeannette and I ran away," Lisa says. "She and I ended up getting into a fight. Like a *real* fight; punches thrown and everything. Jeannette was tough. We beat each other up real good." Lisa recalls Florence DePalma's shock and dismay upon picking up the two cousins. "She was convinced that we had been raped. She kept yelling, 'Did you get raped?! Tell me!' and we just laughed it off. There was no telling her; she was absolutely convinced of it."

While Lisa does acknowledge the rebellious and particularly dangerous aspect of her and her cousin's behavior, she is quick to point out that just as much time was spent volunteering for their church. "Jeannette and I did Christian outreach work for the Evangel Church in Elizabeth," she says proudly. "We used to spend hours walking all around Elizabeth, handing out fliers and preaching the word of the Lord. Jeannette loved doing God's work. We were just these little hippies trying to teach people about Jesus," she fondly recalls with a smile.

"She never mentioned to me that she was religious or devoted to a Christian lifestyle," Grace Petrilli DiMuro, a high school friend of Jeannette's, recalls. "Although, if being a good Christian meant being a good friend, looking out for you, helping you if she could, that's what I saw." Grace and Jeannette had met sometime in 1970, when the two were freshmen at Jonathan Dayton Regional High School in Springfield. Jeannette had transferred from Union Catholic Regional High School in Scotch Plains to Jonathan Dayton Regional High School in Springfield at some point during this time. While the definitive reason remains unknown, several theories abound.

"The impression that we had was that Jeannette's mother was convinced of her daughter's religious nature and had removed her from Union Catholic because the 'kids in public school needed her example more,'" Margaret Bandrowski recalls.

Cindy DePalma has a different opinion on the matter: "I don't remember exactly when or why Jeannette transferred from Union Catholic to Jonathan Dayton, but it could have been the traveling distance, or maybe she just wanted to go to Dayton."

"The thing about Jeannette was this: when you first saw her, you assumed this preconceived notion of her being this tough, fast, wild girl," Grace Petrilli DiMuro continues. "But when you would start talking to her, she was so sweet, honest and funny. Some of the other girls in our grade weren't so friendly to her because of that. These girls wouldn't make any effort to be friendly with her. If Jeannette tried to be friendly with them, they would ignore her."

A factor in Jeannette's social isolation might have been her perceived attitude. Grace remembers Jeannette rarely smiling, often walking the halls with an intense, contemplative look on her face. "That was her expression all the time. She only smiled if she said or heard something funny, but it was never really a full smile. Even her sister Cindy never had like a pleasant look on her face."

One of two Jonathan Dayton sophomores who were interviewed for the October

Jeannette DePalma's 1971 Jonathan Dayton High School portrait. *Courtesy of the DePalma family.*

4, 1972 edition of the *Elizabeth Daily Journal* had similar recollections. "She never talked much," the student was quoted as saying. "You had to lead the conversation." The student also recalled that he and Jeannette talked only about their respective classes during their study hall conversations; he explicitly recalled the topic of religion never being brought up. Jeannette's unique choice of attire also stood out in this pupil's memory. The classmate told the *Elizabeth Daily Journal* that the "most remarkable" thing about Jeannette was a black corduroy jacket that she often wore—one that featured a bright display of bursting rainbows on the back. Jeannette's study hall companion mentioned having never seen a jacket like the one she wore until another student began wearing one the following school year.

A fellow pupil at Jonathan Dayton also recalls Jeannette's supposed unusual demeanor. "If she was walking down the hallway, she looked almost surly," recalls the former classmate, who has asked not to be named. "She came off as unapproachable. I don't think her home or family life was that

Springfield's Jonathan Dayton High School in 2013. Jeannette DePalma was preparing for her junior year at Dayton when her life was tragically cut short. *Photo by Jesse P. Pollack.*

great. It just didn't look like she came from a good home. You know when you see a happy family and the kids look like they must come from a good home? I just didn't get that from her. It seemed like she came and went and really didn't have to answer to anyone about where she was going. I guess this is why I almost felt like 'why am I surprised?' when I heard what had happened to her…"

Grace Petrilli DiMuro understands the impressions that her classmates had of Jeannette yet insists that she was, at heart, a kind and sensitive person. "She was very sweet, but she didn't take anyone's crap. She didn't necessarily start trouble, but she wouldn't back down if someone started with her. Still, with all of that in mind, when Jeannette showed you her vulnerable side, you were seeing the real Jeannette."

Jeannette's vulnerable nature, along with her inherent insecurity, often manifested itself through her habit of constantly brushing her hair. Melissa Benner remembers Jeannette "never being without a hairbrush." The young, attractive teenager was often seen compulsively brushing her long brunette locks several times a day. "Straight hair was the style back then," Melissa recalls. "Jeannette's hair was curly, so she was always trying to flatten out the curls."

When asked if she recalls Jeannette's constant habit of trying to straighten her hair, Grace Petrilli DiMuro laughs. "Yes! She was doing that all the time!" she says with a smile. "If she wasn't brushing it, she was trying to smooth it out with her hands, or she was pulling the two sides from the back to the front and pulling on them like they were braids. Her hair was frizzy and wavy, but it wasn't particularly thick or anything. That's the kind of stuff that she would ask me about because I had long, straight hair back then. I remember I told her to use the 'two cans trick' and wrap the rest of her hair around her head to get it straight. She thought that was hilarious! She would often come to me for advice."

Gail Donohue, too, remembers Jeannette's desire for straighter hair. "Straight hair was the thing in those days," she recalls. "We had the curliest hair in the world. We used to blow dry our hair and put it up with a big orange juice can. All society looked at, at that point, was straight hair. Now, you can do anything you want. Of course, New Jersey is humid, and our straightened hair would last maybe fifteen minutes to a half hour."

Despite Grace Petrilli DiMuro's memories of Jeannette's sweet and vulnerable side, she does acknowledge that some of the "preconceived notions" of Jeannette's "wild" nature were, indeed, accurate. "She was a little on the wild side. Because of this, we only hung out in school and not after. She had told me a few things about boys and drugs, but I was a little more reserved."

At school, the two girls often sat together in study hall, engrossed in conversation. "Jeannette didn't talk about goals or life plans, just short-term stuff like where she was going that weekend," Grace laughs.

"She probably would have wanted to be a rock star," says Gail Donohue.

"We were both Italian, so we talked about our families a lot," Grace continues. "We'd talk about music, too. She loved Janis Joplin." Grace remembers one particular afternoon in study hall when Jeannette was uncharacteristically upset. When Grace asked her what was wrong, Jeannette told her that she had just been told that a favorite actor of hers, Pete Duel, had recently killed himself. Duel had achieved popular recognition by portraying the outlaw character of Hannibal Heyes on the hit ABC television series *Alias Smith and Jones*. On New Year's Eve 1971, the actor famously committed suicide by shooting himself in the head with a revolver at his Hollywood Hills home.

In modern society, the idea of a teenager being labeled "wild" and shunned for listening to rock music and recreational marijuana use seems almost alien. Perhaps even laughable. The recollections of Grace Petrilli

DiMuro and Lisa Treich Greulich seem to portray Jeannette DePalma as an average rebellious teenager—certainly by today's standards. Other members of her inner circle, however, have more ominous memories.

"Jeannette's mother told me that her daughter was reading a book on Satanism," says Pastor James Tate of Cranford New Jersey's Calvary Tabernacle Church. Tate first became acquainted with the DePalma family at the Assemblies of God Evangel Church in Elizabeth, New Jersey, in the early 1970s. "The DePalmas came to our church during the season that we in spiritual circles like to call 'the Jesus movement,'" Pastor Tate recalls.

Beginning in the late 1960s, the Jesus movement originated as an offshoot of the anti-establishment counterculture that had taken the West Coast of the United States by storm and had been steadily spreading across the country as the war in Vietnam raged on. The Jesus movement soon found a home in disenchanted hippies who were looking for further spiritual enlightenment. Teenagers and young adults who had once pledged allegiance to Timothy Leary and Ken Kesey were now seeking a simpler and more satisfying existence, similar to the lives of the early Christians. The movement eventually gained prominence and notoriety as a result of nationwide media attention. Followers of the Jesus movement were labeled as "Jesus people" by those who were sympathetic to their cause. Their detractors, however, reveled in branding these young disciples as "Jesus freaks." In what was perhaps a prime example of the Christian ethos of "turning the other cheek," these followers happily embraced the "Jesus freak" nomenclature as a symbol of positive self-identification.

One particular family in Springfield Top had become enamored of this new boom in spiritual culture and offered to bring their young neighbor Cindy DePalma along to the Assemblies of God Evangel Church for a Sunday service. Florence and Salvatore DePalma's youngest child quickly became captivated by this new congregation. Before long, the rest of the once-devout Roman Catholic family began attending services in Elizabeth several times a week. The DePalmas soon declared themselves to be born-again Evangelical Christians. In a conservative community largely composed of Italian American Roman Catholics, this new revelation brought further negative attention to Jeannette's family.

"The DePalma family were definitely in the frontlines of the born-again Christianity movement," Gail Donohue says. "But I think the skepticism regarding that family was more of a social skepticism in the sense that, if you and your wife might say, 'Hey let's call so-and-so and so-and-so and have everybody bring hors d'oeuvres and we'll all just have a cocktail party before dinner'—that relationship did not exist between the DePalma family and their neighbors. I hate to sound like a snob, but I guess the people of that neighborhood might have felt that the DePalmas were not the right people for that neighborhood. I don't mean that in a mean way, I just mean that honestly. It was a kind of socioeconomic snobbery."

Mary Starr,* a former neighbor of the DePalmas, can recall another unsettling reason for the aversion that the neighborhood felt toward Jeannette's family. "You need to understand that Jeannette's father was very much involved with the Mafia," Starr says. "He was a local *capo*. It was an open secret. We knew who was in the Cosa Nostra, but we never talked about it. To be honest with you, Mountainside was a fairly heavy Mafia town. I did speculate and wonder if what happened to her was some sort of Mafia-related retaliation. We were very cautious. We had the DePalmas living nearby and another family in Mountainside that was very involved with the Mafia. This other family was either involved with 'Gyp' DeCarlo and the Genovese family or the Gambino family. We heard all kinds of rumors about bodies on hooks and things like that, so we were very careful. They were not the nicest people in the world. They were mean, from my perspective, at least. They were bullies. They were very cruel to my siblings and myself, so we really had very little to do with them."

"They were the black sheep family of Springfield," Roy Simpson says. "This is innuendo from what the neighborhood talk was at the time, but they were considered to be kind of a tough family. The girls were always kind of considered to be a little bit more on the sleazy side, which is a terrible thing to say, but that was the gossip in the area at the time."

Mary Starr agrees with this gossip. "Jeannette dated a lot," she says. "I would definitely say that she was a wild child. I remember there being a series of boyfriends. We would see cars coming up the street for Jeannette and Gwendolyn. They all smoked cigarettes and things like that. I think Jeannette was more into experimentation than a lot of the other kids in high school."

Gail Donohue, however, downplays the rumors regarding her best friend's supposed promiscuity. "I know she liked to kiss," she says. "But in that day and age, it was first base, maybe second, and that was it. She was a virgin."

"I didn't find out until much later after the incident, but I had heard that Jeannette had gotten religious toward the end," Simpson continues. "What we in the neighborhood remember is her wild side. I can tell you firsthand that we never saw the religious side of her or heard anything about it during the time that this all was happening. None of us remember that part of it. I didn't even hear about it until years and years afterward when I actually read it somewhere. It was not common knowledge in the neighborhood. The DePalma family was always kind of looked at as a tough, hard-nosed kind of family."

In 2004, a man who identified himself simply as "Rich" granted an interview to *Weird NJ* magazine. During the course of that interview, Rich spoke at length about Jeannette and the services that the DePalma family attended at the Assemblies of God Evangel Church in Elizabeth: "It was a very weird church [Jeannette] went to. My friend met her at a high school dance. He kind of fell head over heels for her. She was really cute. He said, 'When can I see you again?' And she said, 'My parents are very strict; the only way you can see me is if you come to church with me.' She was a really cute girl, a girl that guys would really like, and she had a really charming way about her. She was kind of a little bit of a wild girl. I don't think she was so religious so much as she was dragged by her parents to church. She was a girl who was just very rebellious. She didn't want to be dragged to that church three times a week. It wasn't just a Sunday service."

Cindy DePalma refutes that notion. "We were not forced," she insists.

Gail Donohue, however, agrees with Rich's assessment. "I felt like she was pressured," she says. "I remember being down the shore with Jeannette about two weeks before she vanished. We were down at Wildwood for my birthday, and in order for Jeannette and I to be able to go out on the boardwalk and play some games and look for some boys, we had to tell their parents that we were going out to 'witness.' Now, I'm a lapsed Roman Catholic, so I didn't know anything about this stuff. That was the lie that we told her parents. We said we were handing out the Bible and stuff. I know she felt pressured about the witnessing thing. I mean, here we are at sixteen years old on the boardwalk distributing these witnessing pamphlets. I knew nothing about this stuff."

Rich continued his interview with *Weird NJ* magazine by saying the following:

[My friend] *was so smitten with her that he did go to church with her.* [He] *came back and told us and said, "Hey, go to this service, it's really wild. And besides, the chicks running around are really cute." So, that's why we went. It was a really wild Pentecostal, really intense service she went to. Faith healing, all that stuff went on in that church. I would say that I knew Jeannette for about four months before she died. All of us got to know her and the church pretty well. There were several unusual things about it. It was a church in the middle of Elizabeth, which is a rundown area, yet all the people in the church were very white collar, from Springfield,*

Summit; very white in a lower economic area. Most Pentecostals are from down south or black. We stuck out like a sore thumb. We looked like the Rolling Stones in the back of a white collar Pentecostal church. Most upper class people do not become Pentecostals. White upper middle class people, they usually go to those conservative churches, like Methodists and Catholic. But what were all these guys? Well-heeled people sitting with their kids in the middle of Elizabeth, listening to miracle services and getting very involved with it.

The services were electrifying. My friends and I sat there in the services half the time with our jaws dropped. [My friends and I] *were all Catholics. You know the way the Catholic mass is; the Catholic priest is not very demonstrative. We were sitting in this church, and all kinds of weird, and heavy, heavy hellfire and brimstone preaching. And the people that went there kind of had a glassy-eyed look, now that I look back on it.*

This was around '72, and me and my friends were kind of long-haired hippies, trying to get after the girls in the church, and that's why we were there. But what we saw when we were there, it was really weird. Honest to God, I didn't know if we were watching something holy or demonic.

Imagine being a kid who's ten, eleven years old, and a lot of the kids were, and like I said, they were all white, middle class, with their parents. They're hearing preaching that would scare the bejesus out of you. The preacher was up there like, "If you don't accept Jesus as your savior, you'll burn in eternal hell. The smoke of your torment will go up forever!" That kind of stuff. Electrifying! This was no Catholic service. This was a real Pentecostal, wild demons getting thrown out of people. The pastor would touch his hand on somebody's forehead and you'd hear like a growl of a demon coming out of a guy. And then he would fall down and say, "Oh my God, I've been delivered! Satan is out of me!" That kind of stuff. A lot of churches have "accept Christ as your savior," and there's nothing wrong with that, but this was a step beyond. People were talking in tongues, and they used to try and preach to me and my friends all the time, yet they had this glassy-eyed kind of farawayness. Kind of like the way Moonies might be perceived.

We just had a bad feeling in that church, although at that time I didn't recognize it. At this time, when I was only nineteen, I didn't put all these pieces together. But, I'm thinking, "Man, that was a weird situation Jeannette was in when this happened." I didn't think anything so Christian could have ties to Satanism. But, I was studying the Bible for years, and there are those denominations where you just don't know if you're seeing the work of Christ or of the Devil.

If I was talking to a detective, I'd say, "Look in the direction of that church, it was weird," and if I was a detective myself, I would actually look at who was the pastor in the 1970s and what happened to him. The weirdest feeling I have is that maybe that had something to do with such a bizarre death. And she was such a pure type in a lot of ways, she would be somebody that Satanic people would go after.

Jeannette's nephew John Bancey was interviewed for the same issue of *Weird NJ* magazine. During his interview, Bancey criticized Rich's assessment of the then Reverend Tate's church. "I've been there many times," Bancey told *Weird NJ.* "It was Evangelical. It had youth groups. You could trust people. We'd go to youth groups and stuff like that. They'd have the big sermon on Sunday. My grandfather was a big contributor to the church." Bancey, in particular, refuted Rich's notion of the Assemblies of God Evangel Church practicing faith healing. "That's a whole different class. You're talking about like the Pentecostal Holiness Church. They do weird stuff. This is more like a Baptist church." While Bancey refuted Rich's memories of the church having Pentecostal qualities, he did acknowledge the then Reverend Tate's sometimes damning sermons. "Well yeah, it's like 'You'll burn...' and stuff like that, but it was a very mellow church."

Another parishioner, Joseph Cosentino,* remembers Tate's animated style of preaching, but his recollections tend to give more corroboration to Rich's account than John Bancey's. "There was nothing mellow about it," Cosentino says. "This was a big church. It was like Benny Hinn. They used to bring in guest pastors and all this kind of crap. They'd yell and scream and jump up and down. There was faith healing and speaking in tongues. They did that all the time. Tongues, faith healing, baptisms, demon castings, lots of people giving their lives and 10 percent of their earnings to Jesus. It was quite the show, really. I never thought of it as evil or anything—just a really overblown, weird church. Looking back, it was like some of the parishioners were almost using their daughters to get young guys to come to the church and give money to it. Kind of odd when you think about it—an outreach program from a church full of rich people comes into an inner-city park to recruit a bunch of drug-soaked *heads*? Most of us had money for pot and LSD, but church? Not to be anything other than honest, they did have some fine-looking daughters, but most people from their neighborhoods would be appalled to have any of us show up at their own church. I remember thinking that was a little odd at the time. I hung around that church long enough to know what a load of shit it was and got out of there pretty quick. After a while, I just asked myself what the hell I was doing there. It was not anything that I believed in. I don't know about corruption or who was pocketing the money, but the whole thing wasn't like a Christian church. It was evangelistic. I went there for about three or four months. I saw the hypocrisy, and I had to walk away from it. It was just one of those places where a lot of rich people went. They all tried to *out-rich* each other. Their idea of doing good was donating money when Pastor Tate needed a new van. I thought it was silly. These people didn't believe in God; they believed in getting people's money. The whole thing was a show. I decided that if I wanted to see a show, I was going to pay ten bucks to see Led Zeppelin instead of watching Pastor Tate get up there, getting all sweaty and excited about some bullshit that I didn't even believe in. I didn't come from a rich family or anything like that. I grew up in Newark—*a shithole*. The last few months that I was there, I would just stop in every now and then just to say hi to some friends I had there."

During his short time attending services at the Assemblies of God Evangel Church, Cosentino became acquainted with the DePalma family. "I knew Jeannette and her sisters Cindy and Gwendolyn. I knew her mom and dad, too, actually. I had dinner over their house a couple of times. I hadn't seen Jeannette for probably a year prior to her death. By then, I was completely out of that whole scene." Cosentino has since heard of Jeannette's reputation of being a "wild child" but disputes its accuracy. "If Jeannette was 'wild,' I knew nothing about that," he insists. "Cindy and Gwendolyn were both pretty hard, but Jeannette was definitely not like that at all. She was their sister, and you could tell that they were similar in a lot of ways, but she was pretty sweet."

By 1972, the term "Jesus freak" had become a household name in America, and by Lisa Treich Greulich's own account, she and her cousin Jeannette had become full-fledged Jesus freaks themselves. Pastor Tate, however, does not share this sentiment.

"Jeannette attended services, but I don't think I could say that her interests were really in Jesus so much as her involvement in the occult," Tate says. "She was definitely involved with some occult things. It's so strange that she wanted to be involved with that, especially when her family was getting so involved with the Lord. Knowing her, it probably was an act of rebellion. She was a very rebellious girl."

Cindy DePalma, however, denies Pastor Tate's allegations of Jeannette being involved in occult activity. "There were no witchcraft books," she

Jeannette, Cindy and Gwendolyn DePalma, circa 1970. *Courtesy of the DePalma family.*

maintains. "Jeannette and I were afraid of the devil. I don't remember any strange books being found at all."

Gail Donohue also doubts the veracity of Pastor Tate's claims. "I don't remember Jeannette ever having an interest in the occult," she says. "You know, but at that age, it's possible because kids like spooky stuff at slumber parties and all that kind of stuff. I remember being at a slumber party, and my friends were having a séance, trying to bring Mary Jo Kopechne back from the dead. Her parents lived right down the road from me in Berkeley Heights. We all lit candles and held hands. We didn't use a Ouija board or anything. I was scared to death of Ouija boards. My father had bought me a witchcraft book, but it was so over my head, I couldn't understand it anyway. He would buy me anything to keep me reading if he saw my interests going in certain directions."

In addition, Lisa Treich Greulich refutes Pastor Tate's account of her cousin's supposed dark interests but has an idea of where his story may have originated. "My grandmother found Jeannette's diary, not a book on witches or Satanism or anything," Lisa maintains. "Jeannette wrote in her diary that she was going to stop smoking weed and give her herself to Jesus." When asked how Florence DePalma reacted to her daughter's diary entry, Lisa says, "My grandmother had to have known. It was no secret that Jeannette smoked pot. Either way, there were no Satanism or witchcraft books. Jeannette was *never* into anything like that."

This would not be the last time that a supposed diary of Jeannette's would be at the center of controversy. According to Gail Donohue, Florence DePalma paid her family a visit shortly after Jeannette was found dead. Upon opening the door to his comfortable Berkeley Heights home, Gail's father immediately noticed a book in Mrs. DePalma's hand. She told Mr. Donohue that it was Jeannette's diary and that she wished to discuss a few disturbing entries with him and his wife. Gail's father agreed and let her inside. "Mrs. DePalma sat down on our couch with her funky glasses on and started to read from the diary," Gail recalls. "My parents then sent me away because Mrs. DePalma wanted to talk to them privately. I would say that they all spoke to each other for somewhere around forty-five minutes to an hour and fifteen minutes. After Mrs. DePalma left, my dad came upstairs into my room and had a talk with me. I was writing creatively around the time, and he asked me if Jeannette ever did the same. He wanted to know if she ever exaggerated, or made up stories or wrote creatively, and I said, 'No, I don't think Jeannette even liked to read, let alone *write*.' I think my parents must have been pretty shocked by whatever was supposedly in Jeannette's diary. I didn't even know she had a darn diary, and I was her best friend! The whole thing blew my mind. It made me feel like I never even knew her."

Despite their apprehension regarding this supposed diary of Jeannette's, the Donohue family had other, more troubling concerns. "Given Mrs. DePalma's state of mind and how far out she was, my father did not want me to take any phone calls or have any contact with the DePalma family whatsoever," Gail recalls. "If they did try to contact me, my father wanted me to get ahold of him immediately. So whatever Mrs. DePalma told him that night made him fear for me. He said something to the effect of 'She's so far out there, Gail. I don't want her thinking that maybe she could take it upon herself to have you join her daughter.' Something happened between the two of them that scared him, and he was not a man to be scared. He honestly thought that she might do something to me. He thought I'd end up dead. She must have come off as a crazy person. My father was not a stupid man. He was very conservative. I used to have to throw my blue jeans out my window and sneak them onto the bus so I could wear jeans in school like the other kids. That's how conservative he was."

What was supposedly written in this alleged diary of Jeannette's is most likely lost to history. According to Gail Donohue, her father never revealed to her what Florence DePalma read out loud in their living room that night, and Jeannette's closest sibling, Cindy, has no recollections of her own. "Jeannette kept a diary," she says. "I don't know if I ever saw it, but if I did, I don't remember what it said."

Another tale regarding Jeannette DePalma's diary comes from Brian Paulson,* a former resident of Springfield. "My sister was dating Nick Zavolas, the older brother of two twin girls that were in my class," Paulson recalls. "My sister Christine* came home from school one day somewhat worried. She told our mother that Nick was interviewed by the Springfield Police Department because he was mentioned in Jeannette's diary. Apparently, Jeannette had a crush on Nick and was actually not too happy that he was dating my sister. I don't remember if the police spoke with my sister at all, and I seem to recall that they only spoke to Nick once or twice and then that was it. My sister has flat-out refused to talk about this."

We reached out to Nick Zavolas, who was absolutely confused by Paulson's claims. "Christine Paulson was in my grade, but we never dated. I also do, in fact, have two sisters that went to school with her brother Brian, but I was never questioned by the police about Jeannette DePalma, and I *never* heard that my name appeared in her diary." Zavolas does not know why, but he feels that either Brian or Christine Paulson might have confused him with a close friend. "A good friend of mine *did* date Christine for a long while. His name was Joseph Fantozzi. I'm wondering if Brian got the two of us mixed up. I don't know if Joseph was ever questioned by the police regarding Jeannette or anything, but I know that he did date Christine. Joseph is no longer with us, though."

If Christine Paulson is correct in stating that detectives from the Springfield Police Department were actively questioning friends and acquaintances of Jeannette due to being mentioned in her diary, one can assume that the Springfield Police Department had Jeannette's diary in its possession—most likely catalogued as evidence for its investigation. If that were true, one is left to wonder what Florence DePalma brought to the Donohue residence if Jeannette's real diary was actually in the possession of the Springfield Police Department at that time. The answer to this question may never be known. Florence DePalma likely took this information to her grave.

The recollections of Elizabeth Mullins,* an acquaintance of Jeannette's, seem to lend a certain amount of credence to some of Lisa Treich Greulich's claims regarding her cousin's efforts to change her own life for the better. "I know people say that she had turned to God and steered clear of drugs," Mullins says. However, she is also quick to add, "But not everyone believed that. I don't know whether she was still doing drugs or not, but we believed that she was still hanging out with the wrong crowd."

Another opposing view of Pastor James Tate's recent memories of Jeannette DePalma come from a surprising source: Pastor Tate himself.

Comments that the clergyman made to several media publications in the weeks following the discovery of Jeannette's body do not reflect the recollections that he has shared with us. An article that appeared in the October 4, 1972 edition of the *New York Daily News* entitled "Priest's Theory: Devil's Disciples Killed Girl," featured an interview with the then Reverend Tate, who described Jeannette as an "extremely religious and a very devout parishioner." Tate claimed that the teenager was "so religious that she would often talk to friends and acquaintances about God" and might have been "picked up by someone, or by a group," on the day that she died.

The then reverend went on to suggest that this "someone" or "group" worshipped the devil and that Jeannette might have tried to "lecture them about Jesus; the Person these people detest." While admitting that it was just a "personal theory," Tate postulated that "their fanaticism arose, and they killed her. Her super religious attitude was scorned by this type of people. Witchcraft has become very popular recently because organized religion cannot hold its people. Young people, especially, have fallen away from the church. Jeannette may have been a symbol of Christ to these devil worshippers and that's why they killed her." Tate made similar statements that were published in an October 2, 1972 *Elizabeth Daily Journal* article entitled "DePalmas Say Slayers Possessed by Demons." "Jeannette was unashamed of her love for Jesus Christ," he told the newspaper. "[She] was born again when she realized she was a sinner. She allowed Jesus to come into her mind and body. She loved Christ and preached his word. Perhaps she was drugged or persuaded to participate in a witchcraft rite."

When we asked Pastor Tate if he still believed that Jeannette had been "persuaded" to willfully participate in some sort of sacrifice, he replied, "You know, it seems almost impossible to think that someone would willingly do that. Our Lord died for us, but Jeannette was involved in something that was so marginal, you know? The whole witchcraft/Satanist thing. The occult was, and still is, so marginal." However, in an article entitled "Witchcraft

Implicated in DePalma Murder," which appeared in the October 3, 1972 edition of the *Newark Star-Ledger* newspaper, the then Reverend Tate was quoted as saying, "I'm sure Jeanette [*sic*] herself was not involved in anything like that, but I know that many of the other young people in this area are involved. These kids tell us that when they are on drugs, they are in the control of Satan. They do things they don't want to do, and say things they don't want to say, because of the power of evil."

Pastor Tate offered no explanation for the notable inconsistencies in his recollections of Jeannette's character during his interview with us.

"I am surprised to hear that my dad thought Jeannette was involved in the occult," says Pastor Wayne Tate, son of Pastor James Tate. "I have no knowledge of my dad knowing anything about Jeannette having occult books in her room. I do believe that there was occult activity in the mountains there, as was rumored and widely suspected, but I have never thought that Jeannette was involved in it. She came to youth group. She gave her life to Christ. She was new to the faith and perhaps had some dealings with 'the dark side' earlier in her journey. I know she seemed to have a wild side to her, but she was making progress in her walk with the Lord. I know she said a prayer and asked Jesus into her life, but I am not sure if she ever completely surrendered to him." Pastor Wayne also has fond memories of dating Jeannette as a teenager. "We dated for several months. I cared deeply for her. She was an awesome young lady. She broke up with me because we could not see each other enough. I was in Elizabeth, and she lived in Springfield. I could not drive yet, as I was too young. I was sad about us breaking up and was holding out hope that she would return and maybe we could get the relationship going again, but it was not to be. She was missing for six weeks, and then her remains were discovered…"

The recollections of a former member of the Assemblies of God Evangel Church could very possibly shed light on the differences between what the then Reverend Tate told newspaper journalists in 1972 and his current, more candid recollections. The parishioner, who spoke with us under the condition of complete anonymity, recalls Florence DePalma as being "one who would have ideas of grandeur about her children." The parishioner maintains that Mrs. DePalma "really meant well" but stressed the fact that Jeannette's mother was "not always connected with reality" and that one "really couldn't rely on the factuality of what she said."

"Her mother was trying to paint a beautiful picture," the parishioner recalls. "I guess that's understandable, but that certainly doesn't help to keep the facts straight."

One is left to wonder if the then reverend's comments to the media about Jeannette being an "extremely religious and very devout" young woman were part of a conscious effort on his behalf to not interfere with a grieving mother's "beautiful picture."

The issue of whether Jeannette DePalma was a pious and devoted Christian or a drug-addled "wild child" may never be conclusively settled. The answer likely lies somewhere in the middle. Whatever the case may be, most who were close to Jeannette during the final days and weeks of her life all seem to agree that she was trying to turn over a new leaf and lead a much more positive and fulfilling life.

Sadly, this would all come to an end on the afternoon of Monday, August 7, 1972.

4

THE DISAPPEARANCE OF JEANNETTE DEPALMA

The innocence that feels no risk and is taught no caution, is more vulnerable than guilt, and oftener assailed.
—Nathaniel Parker Willis

Like many other facets of Jeannette DePalma's life, the details of her final day on earth are nebulous, with several differing accounts of what exactly happened or might have happened. According to Jeannette's cousin Lisa Treich Greulich, the morning of August 7, 1972, began in a fairly tranquil way but soon turned difficult. "I was told that Jeannette came downstairs from her room for breakfast that morning, and this was when my aunt and uncle finally decided to tell her that I had been missing for some time," Lisa says. "I had run away from home about a month earlier, and since I had done this a few times before, I guess my family was expecting me to come back. After a few weeks had gone by, I think everyone started to get a little worried."

For whatever reason, Florence and Salvatore DePalma had chosen this moment to tell their daughter that her cousin had been missing for nearly a month. The couple had not planned for Jeannette's reaction. "She was pissed," Lisa says. "She was very angry that her parents had waited so long to tell her. She left the table and stormed off back to her room."

"Jeannette called me around eleven o'clock that morning," Gail Donohue recalls. "I asked her what she was doing, and she said, 'My mom is making me scrub the bathrooms today. I don't think I can come over.' This got me really mad because we had made plans to hang out with these two boys who[m] we had met at Echo Lake Park the day before, and now it seemed like Jeannette was trying to get out of it. I told her to get her ass over here because the guys were on their way. Now, I'm not a bully, but I bugged her to come over because she put me in this position. She told me, 'Alright, I'll hitchhike over,' and that was the last time I heard from her…"

As she hung up the phone, Gail Donohue never once thought that her best friend might be in any kind of danger hitchhiking to her house. "That's when times were a lot easier," Gail says. "Before Jeannette's death, we hitchhiked all over the darn place. That's how we got around. You know, you didn't get your driver's license until you were seventeen and a half in New Jersey, and that was just our way of life. We used to hitchhike to Elizabeth, for God's sake. From middle class to upper middle class, that's certainly how we got around."

What happened after Gail and Jeannette ended their phone call is a notable source of uncertainty and contention.

According to Cindy DePalma, Jeannette approached her, asking if she would accompany her to Gail's house in Berkeley Heights, roughly eight miles away. "Jeannette was seeing a guy named Tommy, who[m] I had never met," Cindy says. "She wanted to meet up with him at Gail's house before work." Cindy claims she declined Jeannette's offer of accompanying her to Gail Donohue's house because of her own romantic troubles. "I didn't go because I was fighting with my boyfriend, and I wanted to stay by the phone," she recalls. "Talk about feeling guilty all my life…"

Gail Donohue, however, denies the accuracy of Cindy DePalma's memory. "I don't remember any 'Tommy,'" she says. "The only Tommy that Jeannette knew was actually *my* boyfriend. He was from Mountainside. Jeannette hung out with, what we called at that time, the 'Greaser Group.' You know, the Italians. This became a problem because my parents, coming from an Irish background, and my father coming from Brooklyn, wouldn't let me hang around with people who were dating Italians in high school. Also, Jeannette *never* said she was bringing Cindy over. Cindy was younger than us; we wouldn't have hung out with her. Cindy DePalma has never been to my house in her whole life."

When we asked for specifics regarding "Tommy," Cindy DePalma could not recall a last name, general description or any other details about Jeannette's alleged boyfriend, maintaining that she had never met him in person. Her only additional memory of "Tommy" was that her sister's alleged boyfriend "may have lived in Berkeley Heights near Gail."

During his 2004 interview with *Weird NJ* magazine, Jeannette's nephew John Bancey recalls his mother, Jeannette's older sister Darlene, once discussing a boy whom Jeannette might have been dating around the time of her disappearance. "My mother mentioned that [Jeannette] had possibly a new boyfriend," Bancey told *Weird NJ*. "He had blue eyes. I don't know how true that is, it's been a long time. But that's what my mother said."

"I also had heard that she was going to see her boyfriend on the day that she disappeared," Grace Petrilli DiMuro recalls. "But, I hadn't seen her all summer, so I couldn't say who the boyfriend was."

Another matter of controversy is the source of Jeannette's employment. In the weeks after her death and the subsequent discovery of her remains, it was widely reported in the media that Jeannette was due to work an evening shift at a part-time job on the day that she vanished. According to Cindy DePalma, Jeannette worked at Brooks Department Store, later known as Sealfons, in Summit, approximately three miles away from her home. Melissa Benner, Jeannette's longtime friend, also remembers this being the case. In addition, *Weird NJ* magazine received an anonymous letter from a reader in 2004 that seemed to validate both Cindy's and Melissa's recollections. The letter read, in part: "Apparently my mom knew Jeannette, because Jeannette worked at a clothing store in Summit named Sealfons. They were about the same age, which should have been around 13 or 14."

Gail Donohue, however, denies Cindy DePalma's, Melissa Benner's and the anonymous reader's recollections. "No way," she insists. "Absolutely not. There's no way. We were only fifteen at the time and did not have working papers. Jeannette and I both worked for a telephone soliciting company. It was up the stairs right across from Summit Train Station. That's where they had their office. I believe it was called 'Handicapped Workers of America' or something to that extent. These people at the telephone soliciting company didn't care that we were underage and didn't have working papers. I later found out that the handicapped people who we were raising money for only saw maybe 4 percent of the funds. I remember, I didn't know anything about the Sabbath, and I called a Jewish person's house and caught holy hell because they're not supposed to even touch electricity. They thought it was an emergency. All we did with our money, because we made so little, was buy all of the candy downstairs, and then we would go back upstairs to make some more calls."

Bert Model, the former owner of Brooks Department Store, later Sealfons, steadfastly denies Jeannette ever being employed in his store. "This woman never worked at my store," Model says. "If any of my employees were ever kidnapped or murdered, I, for sure, would have known about it and remembered."

Whatever the case may be—Brooks Department Store or the telemarketing company—Jeannette allegedly told her parents that she had a shift scheduled for that evening. At some point before she left her home, Jeannette allegedly called a friend to see if she would accompany her to Gail's.

A friend of Jeannette's who requested to be referred to only as "Rosanne" recalls a sister of hers receiving a phone call from Jeannette on the day that she vanished. "My sister was asked by Jeannette to go to Summit the day she disappeared," she says. "My mother told my sister that she could not go, and she listened, thank God. My sister was very upset and scared when the news broke about Jeannette, which was later that evening when her mother, Florence, called my mother asking if my sister was home or knew where Jeannette would be."

After Rosanne's sister declined her invitation, Jeannette grabbed her purse—a gift from her older sister Carole—and told her mother that she was going to walk three miles to the train station in Summit. From there, she said, she would take a train into Berkeley Heights to see Gail. John Bancey recalled the following during his 2004 interview with *Weird NJ* magazine:

> *My two aunts were together, my aunt Cindy and my aunt Jeannette. [Cindy] said Jeannette was getting ready for work but she was going to stop by her friend's house at the time. She worked somewhere in Summit. My grandmother offered her a ride to work and she said, "No mom, I'm ok, I'm 16." She was going to go up to her friend's house and she was going to get a ride to work. My Grandmother said, "You're too young," and she said, "No, I'm 16 now, leave me alone Mom," and that's the last time they saw her.*

After this brief exchange, Florence DePalma reluctantly allowed her daughter to walk to Summit Station, completely unaware that Jeannette was actually intending to hitchhike straight to Gail Donohue's house.

Exiting her front door, Jeannette walked down her driveway and turned left onto Clearview Road. What occurred after this moment would be enshrouded in mystery for decades to come.

"Jeannette stopped by the Bladis home uninvited midday," says John Rosenski, widower of Donna Bladis, a friend of Jeannette's. If this were true, Jeannette would most likely have turned right off Clearview Road and onto Chimney Ridge Drive. From there, she would have turned right onto

The site of the Bladis home as it appeared in 2014. Jeannette's unexpected visit to this house on the day of her disappearance caused significant controversy among her friends and family for decades. *Photo by Jesse P. Pollack.*

Ledgewood Road, left onto Sunny Slope Drive, right onto Sunny View Road and then right onto Summit Road, a large road cutting straight through Springfield and adjoining Mountainside. From there, Jeannette would have made another right onto High Point Drive, where the Bladis home sat on the corner. "Donna was grounded by her parents and was not supposed to have friends over," Rosenski recalls. "Jeannette was not all she seemed to be. Donna's mother, for some reason, did not want her around Donna."

Cindy DePalma, however, vehemently disagrees with Rosenski's statement. "That is a lie," she insists. "Donna's parents liked Jeannette. She was a good kid."

Rosenski's recollections are, however, bolstered by Gail Donohue. "Mrs. Bladis did not like either one of us," she says, referring to herself and Jeannette. "She did not like us one bit. The last time that I can remember being at the Bladis house, there was a party, and Mrs. Bladis kicked Jeannette and myself out. I think we might have brought boys and hid them in the bushes. We didn't go far without boys in those days, but it was a very innocent thing."

"Jeannette was having a fight with her boyfriend and was looking for a ride somewhere," Rosenski continues, recounting the recollections of his late wife. "Jeannette asked Donna's mother to drive her somewhere. Donna's mother refused, and Jeannette left, walking down High Point Drive toward Springfield. This is all I know."

Cindy DePalma again finds fault in John Rosenski's account of Donna Bladis's recollections.

"Jeannette and Tommy were not fighting that day. *I* was the one fighting with my boyfriend," she says, reiterating her original statement.

Years later, Jeannette's alleged unannounced visit to the Bladises' Mountainside home would become a gold mine of gossip and nefarious allegations. According to Ed Kisch, sometime in the late 1970s, a rumor began to circulate within the Springfield Police Department about a party that was allegedly thrown by Donna Bladis and her brothers, Mark and Richard, on the night of Jeannette DePalma's disappearance. In the narrative of this rumor, Jeannette DePalma supposedly overdosed on an unknown or unnamed drug and died at this party. Certain attendees then supposedly panicked and decided to dump her body in the woods off Mountview Road.

"My mother always believed that the Bladises were involved," Cindy DePalma says. "She became suspicious of them when they didn't show up to Jeannette's funeral. My mom just had this feeling until the day she passed."

Jeannette's older sister Darlene Bancey also recalled being told of Donna Bladis's suspected involvement in her sister's death when she spoke with us. "I had heard rumors that she died at party at Donna Bladis's house," she said. "But I don't know if those rumors are true or not."

Denise Parker,* a childhood friend of Donna Bladis, also remembers hearing these rumors. "They say that Jeannette went to a party at Donna Bladis's house," Parker recalls. "Donna always had people at her house twenty-four/seven, but there was no party that particular day. Jeannette just went to Donna's house because everybody would go to there to hang out. She figured that she could probably get Donna to give her a ride, but Donna was grounded. She was always grounded," Parker laughs. "But everybody knows that she was at Donna Bladis's house *last.*"

When asked if the Springfield Police Department ever followed up on these rumors, Ed Kisch replies, "You couldn't get near these people if you had questions or suspicions. The only difference between the Bladis family and a group of mobsters was the fact that they actually ran a legitimate business. If the Springfield cops went to the Mountainside cops and wanted to find out about the party that supposedly happened on the night that the DePalma kid went missing, they weren't going to find anything out. Cops had friends, and they protected these friends. The Bladises were constantly buying dinner for the chief of police over in Mountainside. They had political connections, as well."

Out of all of the theories that he has heard over the years, Ed Kisch believes that the Bladis theory is the one that is most rooted in truth. "I am 90 percent sure that something happened to Jeannette in that house. There are some people who blame Mark Bladis."

A since-deleted post made by an anonymous user on an online message board contained quite a contentious claim: "Mark Bladis told me that he was with Jeannette DePalma the night that she died." A posting this vague could be taken any number of ways—an admission of guilt in the murder of a teenage girl or perhaps a comment made in passing that was wildly taken out of context. After all, if Jeannette DePalma did stop by the Bladis house on August 7, 1972, and Mark Bladis was home, he then truly *was* with Jeannette on the day that she died. Would it be reasonable, under those circumstances alone, to suspect Mark Bladis of any wrongdoing in relation to Jeannette? Absolutely not. However, Ed Kisch remains unconvinced. He cites recent comments made to him in private by an investigator with the Union County Prosecutor's Office.

"Vincent Byron believes that Mark Bladis knew something about Jeannette's death," Kisch says. "Byron did get his nose into that case because he got hired by Union County to specifically work cold cases. A source that I had told me specifically that, as far as the Union County Prosecutor's Office is concerned, that case is closed—dead—and the person most likely responsible for her death is dead, and there were references made to Mark Bladis. Like I said before, I am almost positive that Jeannette overdosed on something during a party at that house. Some kids probably panicked, and then they dumped her in the quarry."

Ed Cardinal and Donald Schwerdt, however, do not see this as being logistically feasible. "It would be nearly impossible for someone to carry her up there if she was dead weight," Cardinal insists, citing the steep hill that investigators had to climb in order to reach Jeannette DePalma's body. "I can't imagine carrying a body up that hill. In fact, some of the cops told us that they could not even climb the hill with the aid of equipment."

When asked if he believes that a group of teenagers could have kept a secret like that for over four decades, Ed Kisch replies, "Oh, hell yeah! Before I retired, I put in twenty years as a juvenile officer, and let me tell you something—kids keep the best secrets there are."

Gail Donohue, however, does not take stock in such theories. "If there was a party, I would have known about it or Jeannette would have told me about

Authors Mark Moran and Jesse P. Pollack in 2014 on the Mountview Road side of the base of the Devil's Teeth cliff. *Photo by Doyle Argene.*

it," she insists. "I don't remember us going to a lot of parties. We used to go to dances at high schools. If Jeannette and I went out for a night, there would be no parties involved. It would be dances at places like Scotch Plains High School or Summit High School, or something like that. I think the Bladis theory is stupid. Jeannette and I hadn't been over the Bladises' in quite a while."

"I don't think it was a dump job," Schwerdt says. "I personally think there was some kind of a party going on there and something happened, and whoever was there with her panicked and left her there, and to this day, nobody knows really what happened. Well, one person does…"

The "dump job" theories make little sense to Peter Hammer, too. "I don't think she was dumped there, but at the same time, she had no reason to be inside of that quarry," he says. "It's all so strange. I mean, she didn't just drop out of the sky either!"

Like many of Jeannette's peers who were interviewed for this book, Ed Kisch does not acknowledge the Houdaille Quarry as being a popular

Abandoned equipment in the woods surrounding the Houdaille Quarry. *Photo by Doyle Argene.*

party spot for teenagers in the early 1970s. "At that time, the kids partied on Baltusrol Golf Course at nights and on weekends," he says. "They had some *humongous* parties out on the golf course. Whether Jeannette DePalma was part of that scene or not, I don't know, but I do remember some of these things could be funny on a Friday night. Don Schwerdt and I were working together, and we got a call from some of the people that lived in Mountainside about some noise coming from the golf course. So we hooked up behind the clubhouse, and we knew there was a party going on out there. So when we both drove out in our cars, we drove out with no lights on. When we got to the area where we knew that the kids would be partying, we then turned on our lights at the last minute while we were driving down the fairway. I've got to tell you, these kids were asshole and elbow all over the place. There had to be fifty kids or more up there. There were more than twenty-four cases of beer up there. There were more than five or six bottles of Jack Daniels. There were shirts, there were pants, there were bras, there were *panties*. I'm looking at Don, and he's looking at me. We can hear these kids scurrying through the brush. I commented to him, 'Oh well, this ought to be interesting how some of these girls are going to get out of here!' So that's where the major partying took place, not too far from where Jeannette lived."

It may never be known for certain whether there was, in fact, a party at the Bladis home on the evening of August 7, 1972. If there was, no one has come forward claiming to have attended such a party at the time of this book's writing. The late Donna Bladis's husband, John Rosenski, maintains that there "was no party at the Bladis home the day that Jeannette stopped by uninvited." Mark Bladis died in 1988, taking any secrets he might have held to the grave, and Richard Bladis did not respond to our requests for comment.

Sometime late in the evening on August 7, Florence and Salvatore DePalma began to feel uneasy. Their daughter certainly should have been home from work by then, and if she was going to be late, she would have called. It was not long before the two gave in to their shared anxiety and began telephoning the homes of several of Jeannette's friends.

Not a single person that the DePalmas reached out to had seen or heard from Jeannette. Florence and Salvatore now began to entertain their worst fears. They decided that it was time to contact the authorities. Once Jeannette's parents got on the phone with the Springfield Police Department, they were shocked and frustrated to learn that it would be a further twenty-four hours before their daughter could be officially listed as missing.

"It was strange how runaway situations were not handled the same way back then as they are today," Ed Kisch says. "Back then, runaways did not garner much attention because they left willingly, and running away from home was not a criminal offense. You know, you put the stuff out on the teletype, but did you really look for them? No. Locally, you would beat the bushes a little bit, but if you didn't come up with anything, sooner or later, these kids wound up coming back home. At the most, you would refer them to counseling. It was no major thing."

All the DePalmas could do now was wait.

According to several Springfield Police Department retirees, Florence and Salvatore claimed that Jeannette had run away when the two reported their daughter missing.

"When she was reported missing, everybody thought that she had run away," Don Schwerdt recalls. While preparing Jeannette's missing person report, members of the Springfield Police Department began to take note of the DePalmas' short and vague answers to officers' questions. "There was talk in the stationhouse that they weren't very cooperative," Schwerdt says. "It was like, 'Let's keep this quiet and not be out in the public with it.' That was my opinion, and that's the opinion that most of the guys in the police station had. The family didn't really come out right away and give any interviews or anything—as far as I know, at least." Florence and Salvatore's perceived lack of cooperation was not enough for the two to be formally considered suspects in their daughter's disappearance. In recent years, the practice of immediately placing suspicion on the parents of a missing or murdered child is much more commonplace, a notable example being the 1996 murder of six-year-old JonBenét Ramsey.

Numerous residents of Springfield and nearby Mountainside also maintain being told that Jeannette had run away from home.

William Nelson, a former Mountainside resident who lived only two blocks away from the DePalmas, remembers the rumors surrounding Jeannette's disappearance. "It was my understanding that Jeannette just ran away," Nelson says. "You know, something might have happened like a family argument or a disagreement, and off she went. But there wasn't a whole lot said about it because it was just another kid who had run away, and hopefully she would come back, you know? It wasn't much ado about nothing; it was just another kid in the neighborhood ran away."

Mary Starr was also privy to this neighborhood gossip. "I did hear the rumor that Jeannette was running away," she recalls. "Jeannette would not have surprised me if she had run away from home. Jeannette would have been more inclined to go against her parents, I think."

During his 2004 interview with *Weird NJ* magazine, Jeannette's friend Rich recalled an incident that took place sometime between Jeannette's disappearance and the eventual discovery of her body. Rich claimed to have been told by Salvatore DePalma that his daughter had, in fact, run away from home during this period of time:

I was not at all surprised when her father told me that Jeannette ran away. She was just that type…they said she didn't take any of her clothes, so the parents were very concerned. She was gone two weeks already when we went up to the door to get her. My friend wanted to see her. He thought she was mad at him. "Why didn't Jeannette call me?" he wondered and he said, "Let's go up to Springfield to her house and try to get her outside to go for a ride away from her parents." So we went up there. Five of us in the car on a Sunday. And he says, "Rich will you go up to the door for me? Because I think she's mad at me, but they all know you." So I said, "Sure, I'll go up to the door." It was an upper middle class house in Springfield. The parents were at the door, and I says, "Is Jeannette here?" And they says, "No, Jeannette hasn't been here for two weeks, we think she ran away." And at this point she was missing but no one knew what happened to her.

Jeannette DePalma in 1972. On the right is her sister Darlene Bancey. *Courtesy of the DePalma family.*

Florence and Salvatore DePalma made no reference to Jeannette's having run away during several interviews that they gave to the *Elizabeth Daily Journal* and the *Newark Star-Ledger*, each time insisting that their daughter had simply left home to visit her friend in Berkeley Heights. After several days had gone by with no word from Jeannette or the Springfield Police Department, the DePalmas decided to coordinate a search of their own.

Darlene Bancey recalled being told by her mother that Jeannette had "left to go to the movies and never came home." Bancey immediately lent herself to the search effort.

In 2004, John Bancey discussed with *Weird NJ* his recollections of accompanying his mother to New York City to look for Jeannette:

I was probably about four and a half, five years old. I still remember what happened. It was in the summer, but they obviously didn't tell me what was going on. Sometime in August. Right before my birthday. In September, before they found her body, we went to New York, we were looking for my aunt. We went all over the place. There were still a lot of hippies and everything. So we searched, and my mother, all the sisters, they handed out flyers, nobody knew what happened. I just remember them saying that she wasn't coming home. I didn't know what was going on at the time, until I was a little older.

The DePalma family's reason for believing that Jeannette had run away to New York City remains unclear. Today, Gail Donohue believes that it was merely guesswork on behalf of her best friend's family. "If you think about it, going back over thirty years, if you're a suburbanite girl, and if you're going to run away—I mean, girls from the Midwest run away to New York City *all the time*. So, I think that was probably a general assumption."

This "general assumption," by one means or another, made its way to the Detective Bureau of the Springfield Police Department. "When the Springfield Police interviewed me, they were treating it as a runaway situation," Gail Donohue recalls. "They treated it as a runaway situation so much that, after a while, I was convinced that Jeannette was hiding or living in New York City somewhere and that I would hear from her sometime. The detectives had me convinced of that. Cindy DePalma literally hit me at the Summit train station because she believed that I knew where Jeannette was. The whole time she was missing, I was just thinking, 'Damn, Jeannette! Contact me somehow, please, so I can at least get your sister off my back,' you know? Initially, for the first two weeks, I told the detectives, 'You guys are wrong. If she had run away, I would have known about it. *Something* happened to her.' It was the constant badgering from the detectives that led me to finally accept that she ran away. Now, I can see why interrogations sometimes end with false confessions. If you're told something often enough, you start to believe it."

While Florence, Salvatore and Darlene focused their efforts on locating Jeannette in New York City, Carole DePalma searched closer to home. "My sister Carole walked through the reservation across from Summit Road, looking for Jeannette," Cindy DePalma recalls. "She never said why she felt this way, but she had this feeling that Jeannette might be there."

Once it became apparent that Jeannette was not going to turn up alive in New York City, Springfield's Detective Bureau began to suspect foul play. It was not long before detectives began to set their sights on members of Jeannette's inner circle. "I know that the Springfield Police Department considered one of Jeannette and I's [*sic*] friends to be a suspect," Gail Donohue says. "His name was Louis. I don't remember his last name, but he lived right at the bottom of Baltusrol Golf Course in Springfield. He was really into music before his time. Jeannette and I would go over to his house and listen to Jimi Hendrix and Led Zeppelin. I think he was probably considered a suspect because he was a nonconformist. He was into heavy metal. He had long hair. I always thought he was a sweet guy, and he was always kind to me, but I think he may have had a couple of juvenile priors. I do remember talking to him and him saying, 'Good God, Gail! They accused me of killing Jeannette!' They hardcore interrogated him down at the police station."

Despite the investigation into the guilt or innocence of Jeannette and Gail's peers, members of Springfield's Detective Bureau apparently failed to locate or interrogate any of the missing teenager's love interests. "I don't even believe that the Springfield Police Department ever checked into, found or interviewed any boyfriends that she might have had," says Ed Kisch. "I couldn't even tell you if the Springfield Police Department, at the time, even *knew* if she had a boyfriend, which I know she did." Although Kisch claims to have known that Jeannette was seeing someone at the time of her disappearance, he did not know this boyfriend's name. "The only person who might be able to tell you that would be Sam Calabrese," he says.

We contacted Sam Calabrese in June 2012. During this initial contact, the now-retired Calabrese expressed a willingness to discuss the DePalma case for this book, but "only in person" and only after he knew exactly what our research would entail. If those conditions could be met, Calabrese said, he would agree to discuss Jeannette and the investigation into her death. After providing the retired detective with detailed information regarding our research and receiving an answer in the affirmative regarding meeting in person, Sam Calabrese ceased all contact with us. Two and a half years' worth of letters, phone calls and e-mails would go completely unanswered.

"That's Sam's nature," says Ed Kisch. "He does not know you, and he does not know what you're doing. Listen, if you were a newspaper reporter, and you came into the Springfield Police Department and you wanted some information, we, as detectives, had the right, through the chief of police, to release information as long as he knew what we were releasing to the newspapers. This way, the chief wouldn't be blindsided because we released something that maybe we shouldn't have released. So, if the reporters came in on any type of a case, we could, if we *wanted* to, give them information. There would be some reporters that would come in and would be very pushy. Guess where they wound up. They wound up *out the door*. There would be other reporters that would come in and could write good articles, and they would be fed a lot of information. I can you tell personally that if a reporter came in and wanted some information, I would ask them if they would hold off writing their story for a couple of days. They would say, 'No, I don't want to wait that long.' I'd say, 'Good! Get the fuck out the door! I'm not talking to you.' They would say, 'You can't do that to me!' I'd say, 'Yes, I can; you're coming to *me*! I'm going to give you information, but I can't give it to you right *now*. You want a story? Come back. *Please*.' They'd say, 'Nope. I want it now,' and I'd tell them, 'Get the fuck out. You'll never get another story from me again.' Then, of course, two days later, they'd call up or come in and apologize, and everything would be fine. There was a lot of stuff that was never released. In other words, the reporters couldn't push for it because that was stuff that was part of a criminal investigation. That was not public information at that time. Now, you have to remember that there are only certain things that are released to the public—automobile accidents, pedestrian accidents, fires, burglaries, et cetera. Very few stories were released. Sam himself released a lot of information to the newspapers, but we could never release the information in our names. The information was released in the name of the chief of police. In other words, there were standing orders. If it was a co-investigation, and the prosecutor's office was involved, we would have to say that we were sorry but we were not allowed to give out any public information and that they would have to contact the prosecutor of Union County for any public releases."

For decades, many believed that Jeannette's unannounced appearance at the Bladis home was the last time she was seen alive. This would have been the case were it not for a recent revelation by Jeannette's friend Rosanne, who claims to have seen Jeannette walking down Summit Road in Mountainside sometime after her disappearance.

"I don't remember how long she had been missing for when I believe I saw her," Rosanne says. "But it was a very profound experience for me. It was later on in the afternoon, maybe even early evening. I remember it was definitely still light out. I was sitting outside on a chair in front of our house on Summit Road, watching the cars go by. I think this was either before dinnertime or right after we cleaned up from dinner. I remember seeing a beige, four-door car turn onto Wyoming Drive and then stop. It looked like an Impala or an older Monte Carlo. I did not see anyone get out of the car, but I think I assumed that the girl who I saw walking toward me from that area moments later came from that car. I really didn't think much more of it until the girl got closer to me. Once I got a better look at her, I immediately thought that it was Jeannette. I can recall my heart beating fast. I stood up, moved the chair and tried to decide whether or not I should run inside my house or try to get a better look at this girl as she approached closer and closer. Although she was walking on the other side of the street the entire time, I wanted to keep my eyes on her. With my heart racing, I tried to muster up some bravery and call out her name. I wanted to see her face when she turned to see who called out, so I yelled out, 'Jeannette, Jeannette!' But here's the thing: she never flinched. *Not one bit.* She kept her head down, almost hiding in the long dark hair that was just hanging there. She was wearing jeans and, I think, a hooded sweatshirt. I can't remember if the hood was up. If it was, the hood would've been a dark color. Maybe dark blue. Either way, she had dark hair and was definitely not wearing a light or brightly colored shirt or top. She was walking quickly, and she did not acknowledge me whatsoever.

"As she continued down Summit Road, now passing Saw Mill Road, I knew I had to do something before she was out of my sight. I ran inside, ran upstairs and yelled for my sister. Nothing. So I ran outside to the screened-in back patio where we ate summer dinners and babbled everything I had just seen to my parents. We ran through the house and out the front door…could not see her anymore. She was already too far away. Of course, there were tons of trees, cars and homes that clearly could have obstructed our view. Today, I would have jumped in my car to catch up and find her while dialing 911, but back then, I recall being frightened and just trying to make sense of what I saw. As for my parents, we were a family of nine, very Catholic, and I was their twelve-year-old daughter running through the house saying I saw Jeannette, the missing friend of their eldest daughter. The same missing friend who was linked to witchcraft, Ouija boards and dark stuff like that.

"I remember asking myself why this girl had ignored me. If she wasn't Jeannette, was it not odd that she had failed to turn her head and look my way as I yelled out a girl's name two or three times? I think it was not much longer that the news broke about Jeannette's remains being found. Kids in the neighborhood were talking about using a Ouija board to ask Jeannette what had happened to her. It was a fad at the time, I think.

"Today, as a parent, I cannot even imagine how horrific this must have been for Jeannette's family and how frightening for families like my own who had lived this tragedy back then. Our town of Mountainside, as well as the neighboring towns of Springfield and Westfield, had some awful crime cases now that I think of it. And yet, these towns were beautiful, filled with many caring families and wonderful memories as well."

While Rosanne's story is certainly compelling, many aspects of Jeannette's disappearance and subsequent discovery do not lend themselves to her account. For one, aside from this single occurrence, no one has ever come forward claiming to have seen or heard from Jeannette after midday on August 7. Another issue is the fact that Jeannette's remains were found clad in the same outfit that she was wearing when she left home on the day she vanished. The outfit Rosanne describes does not match the description of the clothing Jeannette left home wearing. The final matter of contention involves Rosanne's claim that this sighting of Jeannette occurred shortly before the discovery of her body. It is universally agreed among those who were on-site at the Houdaille Quarry on September 19, 1972, that Jeannette's corpse had decomposed to the point of almost total skeletonization—a process that rarely occurs over a matter of mere days.

One matter that is not universally agreed upon, however, is the issue of what exactly was found arranged around the body of Jeannette DePalma, the supposed victim of a black magic ritual.

5

WITCHCRAFT

The belief in a supernatural source of evil is not necessary; men alone are quite capable of every wickedness.
—*Joseph Conrad,* Under Western Eyes

After Jeannette DePalma's remains were recovered from the Devil's Teeth and later identified by her dentist, investigators from the Springfield Police Department were given the uneasy task of notifying her family. "I was over at my parents' house early that morning," Darlene Bancey recalled. "After I went home, the police came and notified them."

Jeannette's older sister Gwendolyn was hundreds of miles away when she got the news. "I was in rehab for drugs in North Dakota when that happened to Jeannette," Gwendolyn says. "I was gone for about thirteen months. I stayed in a home with other addicts, and at the end of the year, they would have a little graduation for the girls when they finished the program. My parents called and told me right away. I was in shock." Gwendolyn fondly remembers her younger sister often calling to check on her progress in the facility. "She called me whenever she had a chance. She was such a smart and happy girl. She got good grades in school." Decades later, Gwendolyn DePalma still struggles to hold back tears when discussing Jeannette. Wiping her eyes and lowering her head, she quietly says the words that have lingered in her mind for so long: "I miss Jeannette…"

Gail Donohue received the news not long after. "I can still remember where I was and what I was doing," Gail says. "We got the notification at

The final resting place of Jeannette DePalma, as it appears today. *Photo by Mark Moran.*

night. I had just washed and blow-dried my hair, and my father called for me to come downstairs. He said, 'You need to sit on the couch.' I sat down, and he said, 'They found Jeannette's body.' At that point, I had no reaction. I went into shock. The possibility of Jeannette being dead had never occurred to me."

On Saturday, September 23, 1972, after a ceremony at the Assemblies of God Evangel Church in Elizabeth, Jeannette DePalma was laid to rest in a Union County cemetery. "Over five hundred people showed up," Lisa Treich Greulich says, recalling her cousin's funeral service.

"I seem to remember her casket being white with gold trim," recalls Tom Hunter,[*] a friend of Jeannette's. "Supposedly, her parents were well off and probably got the Cadillac. Naturally, it was closed, and there was a very good photograph of Jeannette placed on top. It was the picture that was used in the paper."

Gail Donohue's memories of Jeannette's funeral are not of pretty pictures of her best friend, but they do involve her burial container. "It was a closed casket ceremony," she recalls, "On the coffin was a wreath that said, 'Sweet Sixteen.' I got sick to my stomach. I was so disgusted that I literally threw up. I mean, how *cheesy* can you be? To give you an idea of what these people were like, I remember walking into their house, and they had plastic all over the furniture. Look at these people; they made an icon out of Jeannette!" Cindy DePalma, however, maintains that she does not recall Gail being in attendance at her sister's funeral. Donohue continues to resent Cindy for this.

In Loving Memory of

Jeannette C. DePalma
September 19, 1972

Father, God of all consolation, in your unending love and mercy for us you turn the darkness of death into the dawn of new life. We pray now that this your servant, who by baptism became one of God's children and who so often stood to be fed at the Lord's table, may now be summoned to the table of God's family in heaven.

May that Baptism of Christ lead them to resurrection with Christ. AMEN.

McCRACKEN Funeral Home
Union, N. J.

LOVE 404   © ⚓   PRINTED IN ITALY

A prayer card from Jeannette DePalma's funeral service. *Courtesy of the DePalma family.*

Jeannette's closest friend also continues to be perplexed by Florence and Salvatore DePalma's behavior after their daughter's death. "I couldn't believe their lackadaisical attitude about Jeannette's death," Donohue says, still audibly upset. "My dad took me over to the DePalma house the day after he told me that Jeannette's body had been found. I guess by that time, the shock had started to wear off. My dad had called the DePalmas and said, 'May we please come over? Gail is upset and has some questions.' We walked into the house, and Mr. and Mrs. DePalma were sitting on the couch in the back room where Jeannette and I used to watch to television. I said, 'What happened?' Mrs. DePalma said, 'We are at peace. A couple of weeks ago, God told me that Jeannette would be found to the north of us.' They were spaced out. I didn't get the acceptance. It was their child! It was my friend! These people let their daughter go with that acceptance."

Florence DePalma's comments to the news media startled Donohue even further. Only two days after the discovery of her daughter's remains, Florence told the *Newark Star-Ledger* that she had already "resigned herself to her daughter's death" weeks before. "The Lord had given me peace," she told *Star-Ledger* staff reporter Arthur Lenehan Jr. "I didn't understand it, but I just trusted in God, and I still have that faith."

Gail Donohue's reply to that comment is brief: "What parent would possibly say that about their child?"

After Jeannette's body was buried, the Springfield Police Department began to investigate the nature of her mysterious death. Her decaying clothing was packaged up and sent to the New Jersey State Police crime laboratory, and the rolls of crime scene film were sent for processing. The Detective Bureau began to consider whom to interrogate first. During these initial days of the investigation, Detective Sergeant Sam Calabrese and his fellow officers had very little information to work with. A cause of death could not be determined, there were no known eyewitnesses and no murder weapon had been recovered. An explanation for how this teenage girl ended up dead in the Houdaille Quarry and how her corpse managed to lie there unnoticed for nearly two months eluded the thirty-three-year-old detective.

Donald Schwerdt, however, believed that the answer to this question rested with another: where did the makeshift cross and arrangement of stones around Jeannette's body come from? Surely, if those in the Detective Bureau could discern why these objects were there—and more importantly, *who* had left them—the case would easily be closed. The problem was, not everyone in the Springfield Police Department believed that these items were even there. Ed Kisch does not recall noticing any sticks or stones around Jeannette's corpse, at least none that seemed *deliberately* arranged. "She was found lying in the middle of the woods, for Chrissakes," Kisch says. "There were sticks and stones everywhere!" One possible reason for this discrepancy is the fact that, by his own admission, Ed Kisch was in the presence of Jeannette DePalma's body for only "about five minutes," and his attention was focused on locating identification and narcotics in her purse. Is it possible that an officer who spent only a limited amount of time at the crime scene could have missed these objects altogether? Is it also possible that one would have noticed this strange arrangement only if he was attentively scrutinizing the scene in person or thoroughly examining the photographic

Author Jesse P. Pollack pictured on the quarry side of the base of the Devil's Teeth cliff. This is the spot where the Springfield Fire Department was required to back a ladder truck up to the cliff in order to recover Jeannette DePalma's remains. *Photo by Doyle Argene.*

record? An article that appeared in the September 29, 1972 edition of the *Elizabeth Daily Journal* seems to allude to this being the case. The article, entitled "Girl Sacrificed in Witch Rite?" made the following claim:

> *Investigation into the death of 16-year-old Jeannette DePalma is focusing on elements of black witchcraft and Satan worship. A review of death scene photos, according to reports, is leading authorities to believe the girl's death may have been in the nature of a sacrifice. Pieces of wood, at first thought to be at the scene by chance, are now seen as symbols. Detectives thoughout [sic] Union County have been alerted to the possibility that a cult, or a cult member, played a part in the death. A search party discovered her remains—she had been missing six weeks—on Sept. 19 in a wooded area of the Houdaille Quarry atop a 40 foot cliff about 400 yards from Shunpike Road. One searcher said two pieces of wood were crossed on the ground over her head. More wood framed the body "like a coffin." Another person who was there said, "I guess if you were looking for signs, they were there."*

This article was the first publication to link Jeannette DePalma's death with witchcraft and Satanism. It immediately caused a panic and an overwhelming sense of dread, the reverberations of which can still be felt in the tri-state area today. Some residents of Union County and beyond believed that this was merely an example of media sensationalism. Others took it as Bible truth and began locking their doors at night for the first time after reading this single newspaper article. When we interviewed him, Donald Schwerdt claimed to have no memory of any sticks or branches framing Jeannette's body "like a coffin." Schwerdt also said that he did not recall seeing any smaller crosses made from sticks lying near the body, as the *Newark Star-Ledger* reported in subsequent articles.

One person who does remember seeing these items, however, is Jeannette's cousin Lisa Treich Greulich. Over the years, Lisa has made the pilgrimage to Springfield several times in order to visit the location where her cousin's body was discovered. The first time was on September 21, 1972, a mere three days after Jeannette's body had been discovered. Entering the woods off Mountview Road, it was not difficult for her to locate the exact spot. "The police tape was still there, hanging from the trees," she recalls. "There was a black imprint in the shape of her body on the ground. She rotted into the dirt." Around this imprint, Lisa says, were logs. "There was one horizontally placed above where her head had been, and another down by her feet. Her feet were actually resting on the

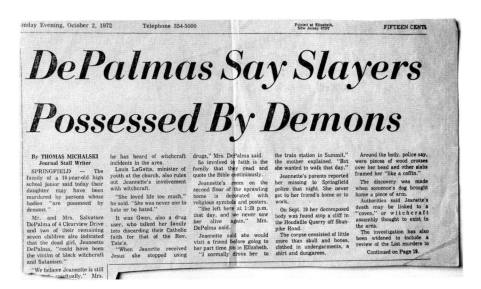

onday Evening, October 2, 1972   Telephone 354-5000   Printed at Elizabeth, New Jersey 07207   FIFTEEN CENTS

DePalmas Say Slayers Possessed By Demons

By THOMAS MICHALSKI
Journal Staff Writer

SPRINGFIELD — The family of a 16-year-old high school junior said today their daughter may have been murdered by persons whose bodies "are possessed by demons."

Mr. and Mrs. Salvatore DePalma of 4 Clearview Drive and two of their remaining seven children also indicated that the dead girl, Jeannette DePalma, "could have been the victim of black witchcraft and Satanism."

"We believe Jeannette is still ___ spiritually," Mrs.

he has heard of witchcraft incidents in the area.

Louis LaGatta, minister of youth at the church, also rules out Jeannette's involvement with witchcraft.

"She loved life too much," he said. "She was never one to hate or be hated."

It was Gwen, also a drug user, who talked her family into discarding their Catholic faith for that of the Rev. Tate's.

"When Jeannette received Jesus she stopped using

drugs," Mrs. DePalma said.

So involved in faith is the family that they read and quote the Bible continuously.

Jeannette's room on the second floor of the sprawling home is decorated with religious symbols and posters.

"She left here at 1:20 p.m. that day, and we never saw her alive again," Mrs. DePalma said.

Jeannette said she would visit a friend before going to her part time job in Elizabeth.

"I normally drove her to

the train station in Summit," the mother explained. "But she wanted to walk that day."

Jeannette's parents reported her missing to Springfield police that night. She never got to her friend's home or to work.

On Sept. 19 her decomposed body was found atop a cliff in the Houdaille Quarry off Shunpike Road.

The corpse consisted of little more than skull and bones, clothed in undergarments, a shirt and dungarees.

Around the body, police say, were pieces of wood crosses over her head and other slabs framed her "like a coffin."

The discovery was made when someone's dog brought home a piece of arm.

Authorities said Jeannette's death may be linked to a "coven," or witchcraft assembly thought to exist in the area.

The investigation has also been widened to include a review of the list murders in

Continued on Page 19.

Just one example of the sensational newspaper coverage following the discovery of Jeannette DePalma's body. *Courtesy of Donald Schwerdt Sr. and family.*

log." Inside this small area is where Lisa found the crosses. "They were little, and they were made out of twigs. They were all around where she was laying." These curiosities were made simply by laying one twig across the other in the shape of a cross. "I could see from the imprint that her left arm was bent under her head, like she was sleeping." This particular piece of information was never released to the press and was confirmed for us by Donald Schwerdt. "I was told by my family that Jeannette was wearing brown leather sandals that day," Lisa continues. "They were like the ones Jesus wore. When they found her body, one sandal was still on her foot, and the other was lying nearby." Donald Schwerdt also confirmed this unreleased detail.

Ed Kisch maintains that he witnessed nothing like the items that Donald Schwerdt and Lisa Treich Greulich claim to have seen. What Kisch does recall, however, are two trees that had fallen against each other, forming the shape of a cross. "As far as the scene where the body was, there were trees that were leaning on each other. The best that I can recall, at this point, is that they were probably trees that were dead and blown partially over by the wind. They were leaning into each other."

Ed Cardinal recalls hearing the same story about the crossed trees. "I don't know if I made it up in my mind or I actually saw a photo along the line, but the two trees were a couple of inches in diameter and a couple of feet long," Cardinal says. "The main tree may have been alive, but the tree that had fallen into it, creating the cross, was stripped of bark, gray and dead. I seem to recall the main trunk having a 'V' or a notch where the cross arm nestled on a steep angle. In the photo I may have seen, or in the renditions drawn that were shown around, I would *not* say it was a cross but something people would want to *make* look like a cross. Don Stewart said he did not see any cross. He was very anti-hippie and despised that culture. He said that the 'cross' was just a tree."

Cardinal also recalls the Springfield Fire Department essentially reenacting the recovery of Jeannette's body as a drill for trainees. "We returned sometime later to take photos of the area for a department drill," Cardinal says. "The drill was composed of bringing the aerial truck up to the quarry to the same spot and practice lowering a victim in the Stokes stretcher, both by carrying the basket and by lowering by rope draped over the extended ladder. I recall Deputy Chief Erskine and Captain Ted Johnson, along with Don Stewart and myself, going to the Devil's Teeth beforehand to lay out the plan for the drill. We did not take the aerial ladder, but we took the fire van and first climbed the hill to the scene. We then drove around to the quarry side where the aerial truck would be located during the drill. I believe we had a human dummy made from old folded fire hose we used to simulate Jeannette's body. During this drill, I did not notice any semblance of a cross or even took notice of the base tree. However, I was not aware of any details of the cross story at that time."

Despite the bizarre discovery of Jeannette's remains, Cardinal maintains that he and others in the fire and police departments had become somewhat calloused toward death and decay. Even the subsequent rumors of occult involvement in this teenager's death did little to alarm the experienced firefighter. "You have to consider that, although the incident had already become 'a story,' the story focused more on the dog bringing home the arm rather than witchcraft," Cardinal maintains. "Besides, I was more concerned with being the fire department's photographer than I was with the overall story of this dead young woman. When you are on the police department or the fire department and you are dealing with incidents such as these, you have to move into a different framework or it affects your mind. There had been about a dozen rather gruesome deaths and accidents that I had witnessed up close and in real time by this point. I had also seen detailed photos that made me—still rather young person—shiver or recoil. There was a boy who had a car mirror jammed into his forehead, a girl who had died in a car wreck because of bald tires, a guy whose head had been crushed like a grape under a concrete truck and a man who was crushed and almost cut in half by a bus bumper but was alive and talking down to the last second. There had also been many deaths and suicides that we on the fire department had carried out of dangerous places, then cleaned up and washed the place down. This was all before Jeannette. You have to consider that all of us did not come upon this one incident as though it was the very first gruesome thing we saw. I am sure we all treated it differently for our own sanity."

While it is obvious that no two people agree on what was and was not found around Jeannette's body, numerous occult historians happen to agree on one matter: the items that were reported to be arranged around the corpse, while certainly strange, were not Satanic or related to witchcraft or Wicca in any way. "There is no pagan imagery here at all and none from any established tradition of ritual magic," says Professor Ronald Hutton, one of the world's leading authorities on the history of witchcraft. Professor Hutton, who teaches courses on contemporary paganism at the University of Bristol in southwest England, emphasizes that the crosses rumored to be placed around Jeannette were "of a wholly orthodox Christian kind. That is the only spiritual tradition here, which makes the comments of the media ironic." Regarding the arrangement of stones that Donald Schwerdt observed, Hutton says that the stones have "no obvious esoteric significance and seem to be there only to frame the head."

Dr. Jason P. Coy, a professor of history at the College of Charleston and a renowned expert in the field of witchcraft, also sees no occult connection. After being presented with a series of diagrams representing multiple witness accounts of the scene around Jeannette's body, Dr. Coy says, "I do not see anything that indicates any 'Satanic' or 'witchcraft' activity. For starters, I do not think there are, or ever have been, any organized Satan worshippers who practice ritual murder, apart from the fantasies of Hollywood writers or sensational journalists. Witchcraft involving ritual murder is practiced in parts of the developing world today in places like Africa, but that does not seem to have anything to do with this case. Modern-day 'witches' or Wiccans have nothing to do with historical witchcraft and are generally peaceful environmentalists and feminists who practice a sort of New Age, neo-Pagan religiosity. Again, that does not seem to have anything to do with this case." Dr. Coy has an even more unsettling assessment. "This looks more like the work of some psychopath with a type of religious fixation," he says. "Crosses have appeared in the iconography of so-called Satanists in fictional works and on the covers of heavy metal albums," Dr. Coy continues, "but they are invariably presented upside down. That does not seem to be how these crosses are oriented. In any case, if some killer or killers were deluded into believing they were carrying out some sort of half-baked Satanic ritual, I would expect them to employ the much more common upside-down pentagram motif."

Dr. Coy finds the social climate of the early 1970s to be very relevant in regards to the media's decision to declare Jeannette DePalma's death occult related. "This seems like media sensationalism to me," he says. "The early 1970s was a time of media concern with Satanic hippie cults. The press coverage of the Church of Satan in San Francisco in 1966 is one example. The Rolling Stones releasing *Their Satanic Majesties Request* in 1967 is another. Furthermore, the Manson family murder convictions came down in 1971. Mike Warnke's 1973 book, *The Satanic Seller*, a fraudulent memoir about his former life in a Satanic cult, launched a major panic among evangelicals in America—and just in time for the film *The Exorcist*, which appeared the same year." With all of these considerations in mind, Dr. Jason P. Coy puts it simply: "I think this is a case of the media jumping to conclusions to sell papers amid the concern with Satanic cults that marked that era."

To this day, Ed Kisch is still particularly incensed by the *Newark Star-Ledger*'s claim that the information regarding the occult items supposedly discovered around Jeannette's body was provided in secret by law enforcement officials. He believes that the catalyst for these rumors getting out of hand lies with the John List homicide case and the overzealous behavior of the Westfield Police Department. "Once a month, the detectives of Union County would get together, and they would share, if they were honest, the types of crimes that were being committed in their communities," Kisch says. "This was done in the event that certain criminals might possibly commit the same offenses in other neighboring towns. Just around the time that Jeannette DePalma's body was found, the Westfield Police Department was working on an investigation, and that was the List homicide."

Nine months before the disappearance of Jeannette DePalma, John Emil List made national headlines after murdering his entire family and vanishing into the ether. A frustrated forty-six-year-old accountant, List lived in nearby Westfield in a Victorian mansion at 431 Hillside Avenue. The nineteen-room home, dubbed "Breeze Knoll," sat only three miles from the DePalma residence. To those on the outside looking in, the List family seemed to have it all. The teenage List children—Patricia, Frederick and John—were even known to flaunt their supposedly opulent social status to their peers. On the inside, however, things were beginning to unravel. John List was a man apparently cursed with an awkward personality. A favorite subject of gossip

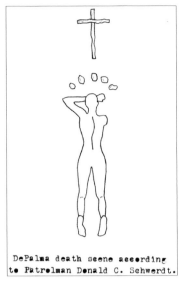

DePalma death scene according to Patrolman Donald C. Schwerdt.

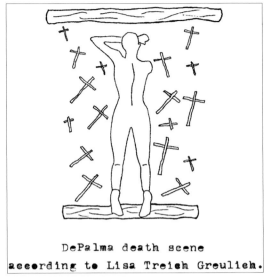

DePalma death scene according to Lisa Treich Greulich.

These three diagrams illustrate the varying accounts of what was allegedly found near Jeannette DePalma's body. These images were shown to several occult historians, all of whom agreed that no Satanic symbols or indicators of witchcraft were present. *Diagrams by Dan Lurie.*

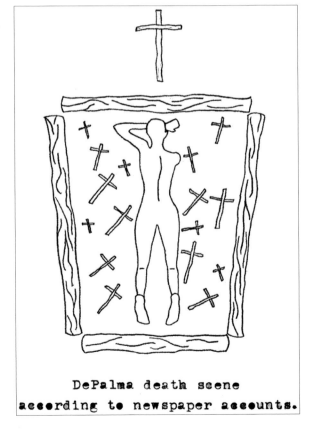

DePalma death scene according to newspaper accounts.

amongst List's Hillside Avenue neighbors was the supercilious man's habit of wearing a suit and tie while performing mundane tasks, such as mowing the lawn.

List had difficulty making and keeping friends and had an even harder time securing and sustaining employment. By the autumn of 1971, the List family was in serious financial trouble. John had carefully hidden from his family the fact that he owed $11,000 on the mortgage, and during his many periods of unemployment, List could not bring himself to tell his wife, Helen, that he had once again been fired. Instead, he would wake up every morning, dress himself in a suit and leave the house as if he were going to work. In reality, he would drive to the local bus station and read until the early evening. Eventually, List was able to secure employment selling mutual funds for the State Mutual Life Assurance Company based in Long Island, but Helen, a lifelong homemaker, was still spending more than her husband could ever hope to earn. To make ends meet, List took out a second mortgage and stole money from his elderly mother's bank account. A man of intense pride, John List could not face the prospect of losing his home. The possibility of having to rely on welfare to support his family was akin to torture.

Another serious issue was Helen List's steadily deteriorating health. John's wife of nearly twenty years had contracted tertiary syphilis from her previous husband, and the disease had slowly been destroying her mind and body ever since. Helen initially hid her affliction from John until after they had wed. For John, this had become a source of great resentment toward his wife, along with the fact that she had lied about being pregnant in the hopes that he would quickly marry her. By the mid-1960s, Helen List's syphilis had ravaged her brain to the point where she lost sight in her right eye and was experiencing severe neurological episodes that caused her to black out and fall. In addition, Helen's personality had become a casualty of the disease. Once an attractive young woman, Helen List was now middle-aged, disheveled and hostile—especially toward her mother-in-law, Alma. In order to afford the down payment for this grand new home, John resorted to asking his mother for money. In return for this favor, Alma would be permitted to move into the small apartment on the house's third floor. List's wife and mother were constantly at odds with each other, often putting John in the middle. Doctors eventually recommended that Helen be committed to an asylum, but John balked at the idea.

In his eyes, List's sixteen-year-old daughter, Patricia, was quickly becoming a serious problem as well. Once an average teenager, Patricia was now beginning to take an interest in theater and the occult—two attractions that deeply disturbed her father. List's eldest child was also actively using recreational drugs such as marijuana and LSD. For most people, the idea of a teenager wanting to become an actor or actress while occasionally dabbling in drug use seems almost normal; the concept is conceivably tame by today's standards. However, for John Emil List, a severely repressed man and stern Christian, the idea of his daughter now identifying herself as a "witch" in addition to her professional acting ambitions was simply too much.

The dark obsessions of young Patricia List may have inadvertently set off a wave of "Satanic panic" throughout suburban New Jersey in the early 1970s. *Collection of the authors.*

The beginnings of Patricia's obsession with black magic began innocuously enough. One afternoon, Patricia's father discovered the teenager and some friends using a Ouija board. List was initially unsettled, but Patricia assured him that she and her friends were "just playing."

If Patricia List was "just playing," it was not for very long.

Soon after, Patricia List began openly telling peers and teachers alike that she was a witch and belonged to a local coven of witches who practiced Satanism. Friends recall Patricia claiming to have had a secret altar located somewhere in Westfield. The teenager also owned a controversial book: Harry E. Wedek's *A Treasury of Witchcraft*, which Patricia openly carried while roaming the halls of her high school. Patricia's drama coach, Edwin Illiano, became concerned for his pupil's safety and mental well-being. In addition to Patricia's bizarre ramblings about witchcraft and the devil, the girl had allegedly told Illiano some disturbing things about her father. During a June 1989 interview with the *Philadelphia Inquirer*, Illiano claimed that shortly before her death, Patricia List had telephoned him to express concern that her frustrated father was planning to murder the family. Illiano told the newspaper that Patricia had asked him to pay a visit and speak with her father but that he was not able to make it to the List residence that particular evening.

It would be a decision that the forty-three-year-old drama coach would regret for the rest of his life.

On the night of December 7, 1971, Illiano and a companion, Barbara Sheridan, sat in his car, parked in the driveway of the List home. Despite being told several weeks prior that Patricia's father would be taking his wife and children to North Carolina to visit family for an extended period of time, Illiano had a feeling deep in his stomach that something was terribly wrong. For weeks, he had driven past the house to see if Patricia and her family had returned home from their trip. The first time he drove by, he noticed that all of the lights in the house had been left on. During each subsequent visit, he noticed that more and more lights were flickering out. By now, almost all of the lights in the List house had burned out.

One of List's neighbors, Shirley Cunnick, noticed Illiano's car—a car she did not recognize—sitting in the accountant's driveway and called the Westfield Police Department. When they arrived on the scene shortly thereafter, Illiano told Officers George Zhelesnik and Charles Haller that he was concerned for the safety of the List family. He informed the two policemen that, while List had called to say that the family would be going away on a trip, they reasonably should have returned by now. He also expressed his concern that eighty-five-year-old Alma List might have been left alone in the home and suffered an injury. Zhelesnik and Haller decided to enter the house through an unlocked front window. Despite being told to stay put, Illiano and Sheridan followed close behind.

Inside, the four were greeted by a very unsettling atmosphere. The house was completely dark, necessitating the use of the officers' flashlights. In addition, it was almost as cold inside the mansion as it was outside. Zhelesnik and Haller assumed that someone had turned the heat all the way down. One further detail made this situation all the more unpleasant. Via an intercom, classical music was being played throughout the entire house. The music reminded Zhelesnik of something that would be played in a funeral parlor.

Upon entering the List home, Zhelesnik, Haller, Illiano and Sheridan carefully made their way over to Breeze Knoll's ballroom. Illiano had specifically requested that the ballroom be checked when the four were standing outside on the porch. Illiano's acting troupe used to rehearse in this very same room. Slowly moving closer, Zhelesnik parted the closed curtain in the ballroom's doorway with his flashlight. Hearing the word "ballroom," the officers expected to find a grand, ostentatious nook of the house. Instead,

Investigators arrive on the scene only hours after the bodies of Alma, Helen, Patricia, Johnny and Frederick List were discovered. They had all been murdered by the family's patriarch, John Emil List. *Collection of the authors.*

they found a cold, bare space occupied by only a few vague shadows. In one corner was a small wooden desk. A cheap acoustic guitar was lying on top. Directly opposite this desk was a large ornate fireplace.

Illiano and Sheridan hypnotically watched as the officers' flashlights danced down the fireplace, past a small novelty pool table and onto a series of lumps gathered together on the floor. Laid out on sleeping bags, these lumps were actually the decomposing bodies of Helen List and her three children. They had all been shot in the head. Judging by the large trail of dried blood leading out from the kitchen, it was apparent that Helen, Patricia, Frederick and young John had all been dragged into the ballroom after being killed. For a chilling final act, the List family's assailant had individually covered the face of each body with a rag. Zhelesnik raced out of the room into his patrol car. He breathlessly radioed dispatch, "My God, there's bodies all over the place!"

Over the next several hours, Breeze Knoll became a hotbed of activity. Investigators from the Westfield Police Department and the Union County

Prosecutor's Office swept the scene, while reporters from the *Elizabeth Daily Journal* took notes and snapped photographs. One such photograph shows a costume witch hat resting on a geographical desk globe only feet away from the bodies. It would later be discovered that Patricia List wore this hat to a Halloween party held in that very same ballroom only days before her death.

For Officer Zhelesnik, moving from room to room within the darkness of the List home brought to mind memories of the film *Psycho*. It would be quite a while before Zhelesnik would be convinced that no one was waiting behind a door or around a corner, clutching a weapon. As the investigators continued to search Breeze Knoll, they discovered John List's office. Taped to a filing cabinet, along with a series of other letters, was an envelope addressed to his pastor, Reverend Eugene A. Rehwinkel of Westfield's Redeemer Lutheran Church. It read:

> *11-9-71*
>
> *Dear Pastor Rehwinkel:*
>
> *I am very sorry to add this additional burden to your work. I know that what has been done is wrong from all that I have been taught, and that any reasons that I might give will not make it right. But you are the one person that I know that while not condoning this will at least possibly understand why I had to do this.*
>
> *I wasn't earning anywhere near enough to support us. Everything I tried seemed to fall to pieces. True we could have gone bankrupt & maybe gone on welfare.*
>
> *But that brings me to my next point. Knowing the type of location one would have to live in plus the environment for the children plus the effect on them knowing they were on welfare was just more than I thought they could & would endure. I know that they were willing to cut back but this involved a lot more than that.*
>
> *With Pat being so determined to get into acting, I was also fearful as to what this might do to her continuing to be a Christian, I'm sure it wouldn't have helped.*
>
> *Also with Helen not going to church I knew that this would harm the children eventually in their attendance. I had continued to hope that she would begin to come to church soon. But when I mentioned to her that Mr. Jutzi wanted to pay her an Elders call. (This is not a criticism of Ed) She just blew up & stated that she wanted her name taken off the church rolls. Again this could have only given an adverse result for the children's continued attendance.*

So that is the sum of it. If any one of these had been the condition we might have pulled through but this was too much at last. I'm certain that all have gone to Heaven now. If things had gone on who knows if that would be the case.

Of course Mother got involved because doing what I did to my family would have been a tremendous shock to her at this age. Therefore, knowing that she is also a Christian I felt it best that she be relieved of the troubles of this world that would have hit her.

After it was all over I said some prayers for them all—from the hymn book. That was the least I could do.

Now for the final arrangements:

Helen & the children have all agreed that they would prefer to be cremated. Please see to it that the costs are kept low.

For Mother, she has a plot at the Frankenmuth church cemetary [sic]. *Please contact:*

Mr. Herman Schellhas

Rt. 4

Vassar, Mich., 41768

(She always wanted Rev. Herman Zelinder of Bay City to preach the sermon. But he's not well.)

He's married to a niece of Mothers & knows what arrangements are to be made.

Also I'm leaving some letters in your care. Please send them on & add whatever comments you think appropriate.

The relationships are as follows:

Mrs. Lydia Meyer—Mothers sister

Mrs. Eva Morris—Helens mother

Jean Syfert—Helens sister

~~Fred & Clara—John sponsor~~

~~Herb & Ruth—Freds sponsor~~

~~Marie—Pats sponsor~~

Also I don't know what will happen to the books & other personal things. But to the extent possible I'd like for them to be distributed as you see fit. Some books might go into the school or church library.

Originally I had planned this for Nov. 1—All Saints Day. But travel arrangements were delayed. I thought it would be an appropriate day for them to get to Heaven.

As for me please let me be dropped from the congregation rolls. I leave my-self in the hands of Gods Justice *&* Mercy. *I don't doubt that He is* *able to help us, but apparently he saw fit not to answer my prayers they* [sic] *way I had hoped that they would be answered. This makes me think that perhaps it was for the best as far as the childrens* [sic] *souls are concerned. I know that many will only look at the additional years that they could have lived but if finally they were no longer Christians what would be gained.*

Also, I'm sure many will say "How could anyone do such a horrible thing."—My only answer is it isn't easy and was only done after much thought.

Pastor Mrs. Morris may be reached at

> *802 Pleasant Hill Dr.*
> *Elkin—Home of her sister.*

One other thing. It may seem cowardly to have always shot from behind but I didn't want any of them to know even at the last second that I had to do this to them.

John got hurt more because he seemed to struggle longer. The rest were immediately out of pain. John ~~probably~~ didn't consciously feel anything either.

Please remember me in your prayers I will need them whether or not the government does its duty as it see [sic] *it. I'm only concerned with making peace with God & of this I am assured because of Christ dying even for me.*

P.S. Mother is in the hallway in the attic—3rd floor. She was too heavy to move.

John.

In the short time that it took to read the five-page, handwritten letter, John Emil List went from inconspicuous suburban accountant to the tri-state area's most wanted fugitive. He would remain so for decades. While her father seemingly vanished into thin air, the ghost of Patricia List would loom large over Union County for years to come. Memories of the self-proclaimed witch's supposed involvement with a teenage coven of devil worshippers would later lead many to wonder if this same group of disturbed youths had murdered Jeannette as a sacrifice. Ed Kisch believes that the Westfield Police Department tapped into this theory and exploited it.

"I can tell you that the Westfield Police Department had talked about finding books on witchcraft in the library of the List house," Kisch recalls. "When I was in the Detective Bureau, I worked with Howie Thompson," Kisch recalls. "Howie Thompson was a very, very good man and a good detective. His heart was always in the right place, and he always kept an eye on you. He would make sure that you were straight. He taught everybody in Springfield's Detective Bureau a lot of things, and he had played, I would say, a pretty good part in the DePalma investigation, as far as photographing

After discovering these bloody marks on the floor, detectives learned that John List dragged the bodies of his murdered family into the ballroom of his home. *Collection of the authors.*

the scene, preserving the evidence and stuff like that. During one of these meetings between the Union County detectives, there was some talk of the scene of where Jeannette's body was found and that there were trees, or there were crosses or there were trees that were made into crosses. I have to tell you—*that is totally unfounded.* If anything, you see, if you have one tree standing up and another tree dies and falls against another, is it possible, if you look at it, that you could see something that nobody else sees? That's a possibility. Howie Thompson was asked at this meeting if there was anything up there to indicate that maybe the people were involved in the occult, and he said no. Now, I will tell you that somebody who was at that meeting went to the newspaper and said, 'Howie Thompson said that the trees formed a cross.' Howie was livid. He was upset because it wasn't truthful. I can remember, after going back into the Detective Bureau and going to these meetings, talking to Howie and saying, 'Howie, are you going to say anything tonight?' and Howie would say, 'I'll never say another thing at these meetings after what they did to me with the DePalma case.' Howie got burnt. He took that hard. After that, he didn't trust anyone. So in any case, there was never anything at the scene to indicate that witchcraft, the occult or anything like that would have been involved in Jeannette's death."

The *Elizabeth Daily Journal* also reported on the supposed connection to the List murders. In the Tuesday, October 3, 1972 edition of the newspaper, it was reported that "cult symbols" were found on the Devil's Teeth near Jeannette's body and that these symbols were "similar to those found at the List family house in Westfield." Neither the *Daily Journal* nor any other media publication, for that matter, ever elaborated on what "symbols" were supposedly found in the List home that would later mirror the scene on top of the Devil's Teeth. One such explanation may lie with the placement of the List bodies in the ballroom and how this possibly could have correlated to the cross or crosses that were allegedly observed near Jeannette's body. If one were facing the ballroom's fireplace, the body of Helen List was laid out in a vertical manner. Her three children were then subsequently laid side by side in a horizontal position to the immediate left of their mother. Many publications somewhat erroneously reported that the List bodies had been stacked or laid out "in the shape of a cross."

One such *Daily Journal* article went as far to claim that the Union County Prosecutor's Office's investigation into the death of Jeannette DePalma had "been widened to include a review of the List murders in Westfield." This article, the aforementioned "Girl Sacrificed in Witch Rite?" cited Patricia List's collection of books on witchcraft, along with the reputedly active coven in Union County, as reasons for the possible connection.

Whatever the original source of the occult rumors may be, the media had done its damage. As far as anyone was concerned, a Satanic cult or a coven of witches had murdered a sixteen-year-old girl and left her body in the woods, surrounded by a multitude of strange objects.

"There were rumors flying all over the place," Mary Starr recalls. "There was a rumor going around that a dog had found her femur. We heard that she was found in the middle of a pentagram and that she was laid out in some sort of a Satanic ritual. I don't know if any of that was true. They closed the quarry for a very long time after that, and there were now guards there. I know a lot of kids who jumped the fence to try and see where it had happened." While Starr acknowledges the rumors regarding Jeannette being an occultist herself, she does not believe them. "Those rumors started after she had died," she insists. "I never heard anything like that while she was alive. Girls in high school can experiment a lot, but does that mean they really think that they are witches? No. When the rumors about what was supposedly found around her body and how her body was found came out, we were all pretty shocked."

Donna Rivera, a fellow parishioner at the Assemblies of God Evangel Church in Elizabeth, remembers hearing the stories about witchcraft being involved in Jeannette's death while attending services. While this gossip was certainly sensational, Rivera was not shocked when she first heard these rumors. "It was not a surprise," Rivera says. "Jeannette was a wild child. She and Cindy were rebellious and a problem for her parents. She was not at church that long before she died. I don't think she was involved with witchcraft. She probably got involved with the wrong people. I think we all believed that was how she died."

While Reverend Tate was seemingly enjoying basking in the limelight that his publicly expressed occult theories were bringing him, other members of the Assemblies of God Evangel Church began to disassociate themselves from the dead teenager. In early 1972, the Assemblies of God Evangel Church helped to found the His Place coffeehouse in Elizabeth. Located on the corner of Elizabeth Avenue and Bridge Street, His Place was a thinly veiled Christian outreach center that targeted troubled teenagers. "The idea was to help what we called 'street kids,'" recalls Curtis Dady, a former employee of His Place. "They were kids who were experimenting with drugs and whatnot. They were getting in trouble, overdosing and having trouble with their families. His Place wasn't the originator or the sole manager; it was just one of the *centers*, so to speak, that did this kind of counseling. The kids from the church and the coffeehouse kind of blended together. Some of the kids from the Evangel Church were from the middle class, and some of the kids at the coffeehouse were more of your lower-class, tough situation–type kids, and maybe they would have drug problems or whatever. They kind of blended together there at the coffeehouse." While offering its own blend of in-house counseling services, His Place also hosted several live Christian music acts. Dady's rock group, The Brethren, was just one of these acts.

A September 21, 1972 *Star-Ledger* article entitled "Springfield Cops Find Girl's Body" was the first public mention of Jeannette's association with His Place. The article claimed that Jeannette "often worked" at the coffeehouse (described in the article as a "community office"), helping teenagers who were suffering from drug problems. Florence DePalma was also quoted in the article, backing up this claim. "They have kids who come in off the streets with problems," she told the newspaper. "Kids with drug problems particularly, and Jeannette would talk to them trying to help them. We've all seen with our own eyes that the kids often find some peace there—and a solution sometimes."

Gail Donohue is more than skeptical about this. "Oh God, do you see what they did with their sick religious minds?" she says. "They glorified her. They made her into something she never was. What credentials could she

A teenaged parishioner of Elizabeth's Assemblies of God Evangel Church stands outside of His Place, Evangel's youth outreach center. Jeannette's involvement with His Place continues to be controversial decades after her death. *Collection of the authors.*

have had at sixteen years old to have been a drug and alcohol counselor? *Zero.* She couldn't have had counselor experience or drug rehab experience in order to teach anybody or to be certified. I know those centers sometimes had people who had demonstrated their recovery working as counselors, but they sure as hell wouldn't have been fifteen or sixteen. I mean, we're talking *lawyers.* How the hell can you tell someone who is in rehab that they've got a fifteen- or sixteen-year-old counseling them. That is *bullshit!*"

However, Curtis Dady provides some insight into this notion. "The idea of a help line came about," he says. "It was actually a network. The young people would be trained just to answer the phones and be a compassionate and empathetic listener, but there was no direct counseling or anything like that. There were these weekly sessions on how to reach out to people in trouble. Basically, if someone called up on the phone and said, 'My parents just kicked me out, and I'm out of money and high on drugs and I'm thinking about committing suicide' or whatever, the kids on the phone would say to them, 'We want you to know that God loves you, and why don't you come down to the center and have a cup of coffee? It's not worth taking your life at this point.' That's kind of a crude example of it, but you get the idea." Dady believes that Jeannette DePalma could very well have received this kind of training at His Place.

However, shortly after the *Star-Ledger* revealed Jeannette's association with the coffeehouse, His Place went into complete damage control mode, disavowing any professional connection with her. On Monday, October 2, 1972, members of the coffeehouse contacted the *Elizabeth Daily Journal* to minimize "the role of the facility in connection with the death of Jeannette DePalma of Springfield." William Edkins, the coordinator of counselors at His Place, told the newspaper that there was "virtually no chance" of Jeannette having been a "counselor for drug addicts, alcoholics or other troubled persons." According to the *Daily Journal*, His Place's staff insisted that Jeannette had "visited the coffeehouse only twice" for "Bible study sessions."

Several of the former staff members at His Place continue to downplay or deny the coffeehouse's connection to Jeannette to this very day. William Edkins did not reply to our requests for comment. Reverend Louis LaGatta, who was the youth pastor at His Place, claims to have very little memory of the teenager, despite previous comments to the press about her personality and love for life. "I really did not know her very well," he told the authors of this book. "She wasn't involved enough with me when I was the youth pastor for me to make any definitive statements."

Alexis Keturwitis, a His Place staff member who allegedly drove Jeannette to the coffeehouse and other church activities, was far more discreet when we asked her to comment on her relationship with the dead girl. "I cannot assist you at this present time," she wrote via e-mail.

Joseph Cosentino is not terribly surprised by the hesitancy of some of the coffeehouse's former staff to speak about any controversial matters, let alone Jeannette. "Something bad went down over there when His Place shut down," he says. "I heard that there was a big drug thing going on. I guess the church split in two because one of the higher-ups was on some kind of prescription drugs, and he was losing it. All kinds of weird shit. I don't know if that's true or not."

It is not known whether the rumors of a "big drug thing" or Pastor Tate's occult theories play any role in Keturwitis's, Edkins's or LaGatta's hesitation to discuss this case. "I did find Pastor Tate's comments in those newspaper articles to be particularly disturbing," Cosentino says. "He seemed to have it all figured out, or at least he was trying to sound like he did. I had heard about the sacrifice rumors—that there were little stones placed around Jeannette in the shape of a coffin or something like that. I think something about stone crosses, as well. Tom Hunter and I did go and visit the site where they found her body. I don't remember how long it was after, but I want to say it was six months to a year afterward. By that time, it was a tourist attraction and easy to find, but like I said, I was long gone from that scene by the time all this happened, so I was not aware of Pastor Tate saying that stuff to the papers at the time. Just creepy."

One person who definitely believes in Pastor Tate's theories is Jeannette's acquaintance Elizabeth Mullins. According to Mullins, Jeannette's company was "questionable," as she was supposedly associated with drug addicts. When asked if she believes that DePalma was the victim of Satan worshippers, Mullins says that she personally believes that Jeannette fell victim to a group of teenagers with whom she used to hang out and that this group practiced witchcraft. Mullins believes Jeannette was targeted because she had drifted away and turned to God. "It's easy to see why she became a convenient target for a bunch of evil kids," she says. Mullins also recalls being told by friends that Jeannette had been harassed by people whom she personally did not know but who knew of her and her involvement in anti-drug campaigns. Today, Mullins claims to be "100 percent sure" that Jeannette's murder was carried out by a group of people, not just one person. Mullins also believes that Jeannette's body was deliberately left on the Devil's Teeth to be found and that her murderers are "still out there."

While they would renounce these beliefs decades later, during the initial days of the investigation into Jeannette's death, her family also wholeheartedly believed in Pastor Tate's postulations regarding witchcraft and Satanism.

"There are worshipers of Satan, and the possibility is there that they killed her," Salvatore DePalma told the *Elizabeth Daily Journal*.

Florence DePalma echoed similar sentiments. "Jeannette may have met her death by persons possessed by the devil," she said during the same interview. "She liked to help others and prayed with and for those whose bodies were possessed by evil spirits. When one prays with such a person, the devil's voice is heard. When that person allows Jesus to enter, the devil flees. There are persons who seek out witchcraft and Satan instead of Jesus Christ." Florence also told the *Daily Journal* that Jeannette had witnessed her classmates at Jonathan Dayton High School "praying to the devil." She claimed that her daughter came home very upset about the behavior of her peers and that Jeannette returned to school the next day to "preach the word of Jesus to the Satanists."

In early October, the DePalma family received a rather disturbing piece of news. On Saturday, September 30, members of the Springfield Police Department allegedly brought a "witch" to the top of the Devil's Teeth.

The supposed witch, who was said to have been a local schoolteacher, was, according to reports, brought to the cliff top in order to examine the "occult symbols" that were found around Jeannette's body. The *Elizabeth Daily Journal*, *Newark Star-Ledger* and the *New York Daily News* all reported on this incident. Florence DePalma was particularly horrified by this rumor, as she feared that her daughter would be resurrected by this witch and not told the truth of her demise. By that time, Jeannette's mother was thoroughly convinced that the persons responsible for her daughter's death were possessed by demonic beings.

Once reports of its detectives collaborating with practitioners of witchcraft hit the front pages, the Springfield Police Department immediately ceased providing any useful information to the press. When confronted with these rumors, Detective Sergeant Sam Calabrese replied with "no comment." Springfield police chief George Parsell was quick to play dumb with reporters and attempted to shift blame to the Union County Prosecutor's Office. "I heard that some people from the department supposedly brought a witch out there, but I know nothing about it," Parsell told the *Elizabeth Daily Journal*. "The people from the county prosecutor's office were also supposed to know something about it. Why don't you call them?"

While Ed Kisch finds it doubtful that any local schoolteacher would identify herself as a "witch" to the police, he does acknowledge that the Springfield Police Department did occasionally consult with and receive help from some unconventional sources. "Calabrese did consult with a psychic on a later case," Kisch says. "She came forward on her own, feeling that she could possibly be of assistance. She offered what she thought might have been useful to the police, which turned out to be nothing. Remember, when the witchcraft thing came out, it was a news item. In good faith, I will say that there are people who claim to be witches—white witches, black witches, good witches, bad witches, witches who practice religion and so on. In a homicide, if witches were thrown into it, it would be a hot item. Let us not forget Charles Manson."

While the Springfield Police Department and the Union County Prosecutor's Office were refusing to confirm this disturbing rumor, one person claimed to have intimate knowledge of its validity: Reverend James Tate. "I never did hear if the witch found anything," Tate told the *Elizabeth Daily Journal*. "But I know she was there." Tate told the *New York Daily News* that a detective from the Springfield Police Department had personally given him this information.

"Judging from the newspaper articles, it seems that Reverend Tate had a lot to say about the witchcraft, as well as Jeannette's parents and family," says

Ed Kisch. "Maybe this was their way of dealing with the unknowns of her death. I can't ever see the prosecutor's office ever believing that witchcraft was involved. Rumors can be very dangerous, and I believe that is all that the witchcraft theory is. The witchcraft rumor sells newspapers, but rumors never solve crimes. Interest in witchcraft is always out there, mainly because it is an unknown, but it is a real thing. There were Santeria acts in the Watchung Reservation. They found signs of animals sacrificed and related it to that."

Situated roughly three miles away from the Houdaille Quarry, the Watchung Reservation is no stranger to rumors regarding witchcraft and Satanism. The reservation, known to locals as "the Res," is the largest park in Union County and a protected landscape. Densely littered with tall maple trees, the Watchung Reservation provided an optimal amount of privacy for those who wished to practice black magic. Unlike the circumstances that surrounded Jeannette DePalma's death, there was ample evidence to support the presumption that devil worship was at play in this 1,945-acre forest.

On Wednesday, October 4, 1972, the *Elizabeth Daily Journal* ran an article entitled "Do Pupils Pray to the Devil?" in which a Jonathan Dayton sophomore spoke of séances that were held on the reservation and said that the son of a Springfield police officer had provided him with this information. The same article alleged that a "number of animal sacrifices have been reported in the Watchung Reservation, but Union County Park Police have refused to comment." In the "DePalmas Say Slayers Possessed by Demons" article that was published earlier the same week, *Daily Journal* staff writer Thomas Michalski wrote that Union County Park Police had discovered a series of sacrifices "involving cats, dogs, and even a goat." Michalski also wrote of a "bowl of blood and pigeons with their necks snapped" being found inside the reservation.

In 2004, *Weird NJ* magazine received an anonymous letter that mentioned the Satanic cult that roamed within the Watchung Reservation. In the letter, this formidable cult was finally given a name. "*Weird NJ* #20 was a better than average issue," the letter began. "Of great interest to me was the Jeannette DePalma case. I was a young teenager when that happened and lived in the next town. About two years prior, there was much talk in my school about the cult you mentioned. They were known as The Witches."

Pastor James Tate corroborated the rumors of this group during his interview with us. "I think that Jeannette was involved with a group of people who would meet in the Watchung Reservation," Tate said. When asked if he was referring to The Witches, he replied in the affirmative. At the time of this interview, Pastor Tate was not aware of *Weird NJ* magazine or the anonymous letter that had mentioned the cult.

"They must have let it be known in the area that they planned to kill a child on or about Halloween, either by kidnapping and sacrificing them or by poison," the anonymous letter continued. "I remember being anxious about this because I went trick-or-treating in those days. I didn't read the newspapers, but I was well aware of the dog that brought home the girl's arm. The story was well known, as I lived within three miles of the quarry."

"I came across a few sacrifices inside the Watchung Reservation during the spring and summer of 1972," Denise Parker recalls. "I found feathers strewn all around. I also saw dead pigeons and a stone bowl that had brains or some organ pulverized in it. On one occasion, my friend Neil and a buddy of his from Cranford were camping inside of the reservation just off of the water tower path. While walking the path, they stopped at this wooden pavilion near the water tower where a couple of guys were standing. Neil walked up to them and asked for a smoke. The guys said, 'Yeah, you can have a cigarette, but you can't look at these chickens.' Neil actually sat on a picnic table behind the pavilion, not realizing what was going on. His friend was trying to discreetly make him realize that they needed to get the hell out of there. Finally, he whispered, 'Neil...they're sacrificing those chickens.' Well, they casually said, 'See ya later, guys. Thanks for the butts.' And got *their* butts out of there. When they got back to their campsite, they grabbed all of their stuff and ran out to W.R. Drive, where they flagged down a cop. They took the cops to the pavilion, and the Wiccans were gone. The next morning, the guys came to my house. I didn't believe their story, so they took me to the pavilion. There, I saw with my own eyes the beheaded carcasses of the chickens. Their heads were strewn about in the woods, not far away."

Parker also recalls hearing about another disturbing sacrifice shortly thereafter. "There was this girl named Liz Blood who lived in a rental house behind the grammar school in Summit," Parker says. "She was around seventeen at the time. She had long, frizzy hair and a tattoo of a serpent on her hand. I did not like her, and I kept my distance. My friend David and his brother Chad lived nearby, and we used to hang out and ride bikes together. Liz Blood would always come around and try to talk with us. I can distinctly remember one of the guys telling me that Liz was trying to talk them into going to a goat sacrifice. She stole a goat from the backyard of someone's home. I don't know where she stole the goat from, but as a coincidence, there was a family in Mountainside who lived on Route 22, and somebody stole a goat from them. It was a family pet. Liz Blood forced six kids to go

Author Jesse P. Pollack stands in front of a wooden gazebo that was used during ritual animal sacrifices inside of the Watchung Reservation. *Photo by Michael Helbing.*

into the woods with her and sacrificed this goat in front of them. It freaked them all out. She could be pretty accommodating as far as hanging out and stuff, but she was always talking about Satan. Then she sacrificed this goat in front of all of these people, and they all freaked out and wouldn't go near her anymore. After that happened, we all stayed away from her. We ran like somebody had a gun to our heads."

While Denise Parker does not necessarily believe that Liz Blood killed Jeannette DePalma during some sort of Satanic sacrifice, she does believe that Blood encountered Jeannette's body before investigators did and left occult objects around the remains. "If there was any Satanic connection with Jeannette's death," she says, "it might have been something like *Stand by Me*, where the kids went to look for the body. I feel like someone might have come across her body, and then word got out that there was a body in the quarry. Maybe Liz Blood went up there and made it appear that there was a sacrifice for a self-fulfilling type of thing."

Lauren Irene grew up in Mountainside during the early 1970s and remembers the Res well. "I grew up on Ridge Drive in Mountainside, off of

Summit Road," Irene says. "The people across the street of us's backyard was the reservation, basically. I remember going to the water tower when I was little. My friends and I used to hang there and smoke cigarettes and chill. My brothers used to go camping up there. There were so many times where they would come home in the middle of the night because they had found unusual, ritualistic objects. I want to say they found things hanging from the trees. The reservation was supposedly a hot spot for cult activity because it was sacred Indian land."

The Watchung Mountains were indeed once home to the Lenape tribe. The word "Watchung" is derived from the Lenape words *Wach Unks*, meaning "high hills."

"I always remember hearing about witches," Irene says. "But who knows. It could have all been just one big rumor spread by everyone playing telephone."

Roy Simpson can recall hearing the nefarious rumors regarding the reservation even prior to Jeannette's death. "I can tell you that there was a lot of talk back then about covens of witches and Satanic rituals inside of the Watchung Reservation. We had heard that rumor for a long time before the DePalma incident happened. After that happened, there were all kinds of rumors that this is what the DePalma incident was about. We heard that she was found with little crosses around her body. I don't know if that's true or not, but that's what the talk of the town was. At the time, it was very prevalent. From what I remember, the talk was that she was found on some type of altar with little wooden crosses surrounding her body. I can't remember, but it seems to me that there was a rumor that there were some animal sacrifices found near her, too. I can't positively remember if that was the talk at the time or if that was something that I heard afterward. As I said before, there was talk about these kinds of things happening in the Watchung Reservation *before* the DePalma incident happened, and after that incident happened, it really fanned the flames of those rumors."

These rumors led Lilith Sinclair, the leader of the Spotswood, New Jersey branch of the Church of Satan, to approach the *Newark Star-Ledger*. During her interview, which was printed in the Sunday, October 8, 1972 edition, Sinclair denied any connection between the Church of Satan and Jeannette's death. "When Satanism is mentioned, many people immediately think of us," Sinclair told reporter Arthur Lenehan Jr. "My people have been getting a lot of questions about the DePalma death, so I want to make it clear we have nothing to do with anything like that." Sinclair was quick to point out that willpower, not "drugs and bloodshed," was the preferred tool of the Church of Satan. Sinclair told Lenehan Jr. that "the power we generate comes from within ourselves" and that her group "focuses its attention on me, and I channel the psychic energy to accomplish whatever the group had decided to do."

Sinclair would later marry Michael A. Aquino, who achieved notoriety as the founder of the Temple of Set, a splinter group of the Church of Satan. We reached out to the Temple of Set in the hopes of speaking with Lilith Aquino regarding her interview with the *Star-Ledger* but were told by Lincoln Shaw, the Temple's executive director, that the "Temple of Set does not confirm or deny anyone's membership" and that his organization "stopped giving interviews in the 1990s."

While Ed Kisch acknowledges the occult activity that was seemingly rampant in the Watchung Reservation, he does not believe that these incidents were limited to just that one area.

"There were also Santeria sacrifices in certain neighborhoods in Elizabeth," Kisch recalls. "Reverend Tate's church was located in Elizabeth. Maybe some of the police bought into that theory and took the investigation in that direction. I certainly don't buy into the witch theory. I must say, on the lighter side, I did hear at one time there was a Calabrese voodoo doll that was in the Detective Bureau that had a lot of pins stuck into it. It must have been true love. Oh well. But that's another story…"

Like Ed Kisch, Gail Donohue does not put stock in the myriad occult rumors. Also like Kisch, she places blame on the media. "I remember when the witchcraft stuff hit the *Star-Ledger*, I called the detectives on the case and they told me to calm down," she recalls. "They came over and talked to me. They said, 'The *Star-Ledger* has to print stuff, and unfortunately, newspapers these days print sensationalism.' They told me that there was no evidence of witchcraft."

Whether or not a series of makeshift crosses fashioned from tree branches or sticks was, in fact, discovered around Jeannette's remains might never be officially confirmed or denied to the public. However, one cross that *should* have been found at the scene never was. A golden crucifix that Jeannette was wearing around her neck on the day of her disappearance was never recovered.

Once Halloween fell upon the township of Springfield, it was hard for its residents to see any child dressed in a dime store witch or devil costume and not think of the dead girl from Clearview Road. While local parents cautiously chaperoned their young children as they trick-or-treated, the Springfield Police Department, along with the Union County Prosecutor's Office, continued its investigation into Jeannette DePalma's death behind closed doors.

6

SUSPICION

The boys with their feet on the desks know that the easiest murder case in the world to break is the one somebody tried to get very cute with; the one that really bothers them is the murder somebody only thought of two minutes before he pulled it off.
—*Raymond Chandler,* The Simple Art of Murder

Sometime in October 1972, a young man walked into Springfield's Municipal Building and asked to speak with Officer Ed Kisch. This young man, twenty-one-year-old Terry Rickel,* claimed to have information regarding the death of Jeannette DePalma.

"I didn't know Jeannette personally," Rickel says, "but I knew friends of hers. At the time, I was actually dating a girl who was accused of hiding her. They initially thought she ran away."

Sitting down in an office with Kisch, Rickel told the patrolman that he had a pretty good idea of who killed the teenager. Kisch retrieved a pad and pencil as the young man began to tell him about a strange figure who lived in the woods bordering the Houdaille Quarry.

"He was called 'Red,'" Rickel says. "He was probably in his thirties then, maybe late thirties. He was tall and thin with wild reddish hair and a full beard. He was a weird-looking guy. He looked like an old hippie."

According to Rickel, Red was a vagrant who often worked at the Baltusrol Golf Club as a caddy. "Baltusrol is more exclusive now, so you obviously can't just walk in there and say, 'I want to caddy,' but back then you could just stand there and wait for someone to pick you out. The golfers you caddied for would then pay you in tips. I think Red had been there for maybe three years. He would live in the woods during golfing season and then go somewhere else that was warmer once the seasons changed." Rickel proceeded to tell Kisch about Red's campsite in the woods. "I told Kisch that this guy lived in the woods right where her body was found," Rickel says. "Her body was found just outside this guy's campsite. It was still golfing season, and he would have still been caddying at Baltusrol and living in those woods. I'm sure the caddy master knew where Red lived, but I don't think the owners of the Houdaille Quarry knew that he was living on their property."

While Kisch says today that he has no memory of a meeting between himself and Terry Rickel, he definitely has clear recollections of the transient caddy.

"Information had come to the Springfield Police Department that a caddy who worked at the Baltusrol Golf Club was living in the woods off Mountview Road," Kisch says. "At that time, the only information about him that the Springfield Police Department had was that he was known as 'Baltusrol Red' and that he caddied at the golf course. After he finished whatever his day was, he would walk up Shunpike Road, then walk up Mountview Road and then go through the fence, where I believe there was a hole. He lived in the woods like a homeless person, or a recluse or whatever you want to call him."

Finally, after weeks of fruitless investigation, the Springfield Police Department had a clear suspect. Donning his jacket, Kisch, along with other investigators from the department, made his way outside to his patrol car and drove out to Mountview Road.

Searching the same foreboding area where he had helped to locate Jeannette DePalma's remains only weeks before, Ed Kisch and his fellow officers discovered their suspect's makeshift home along a creek located only fifty yards away from the Devil's Teeth. This campsite was defined by a small shack constructed from scraps of tin sheeting. Kisch remembers the shack being roughly eight feet long and three feet high. "The man lived in a sardine can, if you ask me!" he laughs. Inside this "sardine can" of a home, Kisch discovered a blanket, cans of food and some cooking pots. Previously cooked rice sat rotting inside of one. Whoever vacated this spot had left in a hurry. "This was where this man was living," Kisch recalls. "He'd get up in the mornings, and I guess he'd wash and head up to the golf course and caddy."

Terry Rickel also remembers this area well. "It was a small campsite. He ate out of cans and read books. He had a shopping cart that he kept in the woods with him. He would go to the supermarket with it and buy food with the tips he made while caddying. He mostly kept to himself, but we all knew him and knew where he lived. I actually knew a couple of guys that used to go up to his campsite to hide out. When he'd come back from caddying, he'd bury his money, and they'd watch where he buried it. When he left, they'd go and dig it up and take his money."

"Red lived in the woods when we were kids," Hank Warner,* a longtime resident of Springfield, recalls. "That's who we really think killed that poor girl; the caddy called 'Red' or something. This guy lived in the woods back then, and you know, if he worked his ass off every day, he could go home with like $120 a day, which was good money back then. There are still people to this very day that caddy up at Baltusrol just because they can get paid in cash, which is king. He lived in the woods up here, and that's where they found this poor girl. I never heard anything else about the story ever since that happened, but us kids that hung around in town, we had our suspicions that Red was the murderer in this case."

It soon became apparent to Kisch and the other investigators that whoever had once inhabited this small campsite was not returning. When asked if he felt it was odd that this man left his makeshift home and food behind right around the time that Jeannette DePalma is believed to have died, the retired detective replies, "I will tell you, there were not too many people who thought it was odd at the time because if there is no official cause of death for Jeannette, why would it be 'odd' other than this was a person of interest that might have some information? Now, whatever the information is depends on what he's going to offer when he's found. Half of the caddies that were working up there didn't want their names to be known because there was a percentage of them that had arrest records. They might only tell you their first name. They didn't work for the golf club; they were independent contractors. They would sit up in the caddy shack, and when they needed a caddy, the caddy master would ring the phone. I think, at the time, that was Don Baker. He's dead now. I don't even think Don Baker was any help with telling the Springfield Police Department who this guy was because he didn't *know*! I think he also only knew him as 'Baltusrol Red.'"

Despite the seemingly impossible odds of finding a homeless man who was known to locals and his employer by only a nickname, the Springfield Police Department forged on. "The department put in a significant amount of effort into trying to locate this individual," Kisch says. "I, for some reason, want to believe that there was even a flyer put together." In the end, the efforts of the Springfield investigators paid off. Later on in the fall of 1972, Baltusrol Red was finally found.

An abandoned Quonset hut only yards away from the spot where Jeannette DePalma's remains were discovered. This hut is now a makeshift home to several transients not unlike "Baltusrol Red" Kier, the man initially suspected of murdering Jeannette. *Photo by Jesse P. Pollack.*

"Out of all this, the man was identified," Kisch recalls. "I can only tell you, if it's correct, that his name would have been Red Kier." Kisch cannot remember if Red was truly a nickname or not. "His first name could have legitimately been 'Red,'" he postulates. One person, Kisch says, definitely knows for sure. "Sam Calabrese knows…" Ed Kisch remembers the then detective sergeant being present for Red's interrogation. "I know he was questioned. I believe Sam Calabrese was present when Red was talked to. The only reason I say that is this: Sam Calabrese was a very aggressive and positive person, and he would have gone out of his way to make sure he was there when Red was talked to. Red might have been interviewed at the Union County Prosecutor's Office. I believe that they located Red's family in, I believe, Georgia, and through that, they were able to get together. When Red did speak to law enforcement, I believe that there could have been an attorney present on his behalf. I believe he came from a family with money. I can only tell you this: whatever the outcome of that interview was…I want to say that Red was cleared and that he was no longer a viable suspect. I was told this was because of the differences in age and lifestyle between Red and Jeannette."

Terry Rickel believes the decision to clear Red as a suspect was a mistake on behalf of the investigators. "The fact that he wasn't there when the body was found is what leads me to believe that Red killed her," Rickel says. "It was still golfing season, so he should have still been there." Over four decades of pondering have led Rickel to propose a possible scenario that may have led to Jeannette's mysterious demise. "Back then, all of the kids in town hung out at the high school parking lot," he says. "When they wanted to smoke some weed, they'd all pile into a car and drive up Mountview Road to Baltusrol Top. Then they'd turn around and come back to the high school to hang out and listen to their eight-track players and stuff in the parking lot. That was like the pot run. All of the kids knew that. I think one day Jeannette decided to walk to town to hang out at the high school, and she knew that there was a lot of traffic on Mountview Road—people she would know. So she walked Mountview Road, but unfortunately nobody came by there that she knew. She got to the end of the road and maybe had to go to the bathroom. She definitely wasn't there partying like some of the cops theorized because you couldn't park your car there. You could walk, but where are you going to walk from? It's so far away from everything. You'd have to park your car on Mountview Road and walk, and then the police would see your car there and wonder what was going on. So I think she probably walked into the woods and dropped her drawers, not knowing she'd walked into Red's campsite. She's crouched down, taking a leak and she sees this crazy-looking guy and starts screaming. He didn't want to get in trouble, probably went over to her and tried to stop her, covered her mouth and accidentally killed her."

Rickel also believes that the supposed "occult" objects found around Jeannette's body were actually part of a makeshift memorial constructed by a grief-stricken Red Kier. "I think she was placed on top of that cliff. I heard that when she was found, her body looked like it had melted into her clothing and that branches were put around the body, like a coffin. I don't think Red intended to kill her; I think he just accidently killed her because she started screaming. I think he put those branches around her because it was the best that the guy could do for her under the circumstances. It was caring in a way. I honestly believe that there were no rituals in the quarry because rituals occur at night, and Red was always there sleeping. There were no witches or cults with the Sabbath going on. That stuff was up by the water tower in the Watchung Reservation. That's where *that* stuff was going on. There was no witchcraft involved in the Jeannette DePalma murder."

Unlike Rickel, Ed Kisch feels that the investigators made the right decision by letting Red go and does not believe that the transient caddy had anything to do with Jeannette's death. In fact, Kisch suspects that Red was not even aware of the decomposing body lying only yards away from his campsite. "The body was up, Red was down," he says. "You're not going to smell a body until you get fairly close to it. If he was fifty to seventy-five yards away, he wasn't going to be able to smell it. It's like coming across a dead deer; you're not going to smell it unless you come within fifty to seventy-five feet of it. That's why I always keep a bag of lime in my garage. We have a lot of deer down by us, and if a deer runs across the road and gets smacked by a car, sometimes they will crawl into the woods on my property. My house is about two hundred feet away from these woods, and I can't smell them. However, if you get within fifty feet, you know it. I take a bag of lime and dump it on it, and in two days, it's gone. So, where Red would have been, there was no way he would have smelled that. There was no way he would have smelled *anything*."

After he was questioned by investigators and subsequently released without charge, "Baltusrol Red" Kier vanished from the Springfield area, never to return. Retired lieutenant Peter Hammer recalls hearing a rumor about Red fleeing to California. Ed Kisch, however, feels that Red most likely went to caddy at another golf club, possibly not too far away from Springfield. "I cannot believe that Baltusrol Golf Club was the *only* golf club that he caddied at in the area. He could have been at Canoe Brook, or he could have been somewhere up in Montclair. These caddies did not specifically stay at one club. They bounced. You have to realize that there's a lot of money in clubs like Baltusrol, Canoe Brook and the club up in Montclair. These are closed clubs. At that time, if you wanted access, you had to be sponsored. You had to become a club member before you could become a golf member, and you could only play so many rounds of golf at that club. Now, I was able to find out at a later point in time that all of these members that belong to Baltusrol probably belonged to five or six other clubs because they had so much frickin' money! They were using these as tax write-offs! They would belong to clubs in Florida, Georgia and South Carolina. A lot of these caddies would caddy up and down the East Coast right about the time that these members would go from club to club because they got along good with the people that they were caddying for, but that didn't mean they stayed there. Some of the caddies, when they caddied, would actually live in some of the motels over in Springfield out along Route 22. They made decent money."

We believe that Kisch is not far off in his assumption. In the early 2000s, *Weird NJ* magazine received a letter from Jean McEnroe that mentioned a seemingly familiar character. "I've got a couple of stories that my father recently told me about from when he was a kid growing up in West Orange," the letter read. "There is a lake in the town called Crystal Lake and he remembers a man that used to live up in the hills behind the lake, which is next to a bowling alley now. They called the man 'Red' because of his unkempt red hair and they said that he used to fish out of the lake and run back up to his shack to cook them. He used to chase the kids and tell them never to go up by his shack."

Sometime in the late 1980s, a body was discovered inside of West Orange's Eagle Rock Reservation, not far from Crystal Lake. West Orange police officers Larry Malang and Ray Rosania responded to the scene and found the body of a homeless man near the Highlawn Pavilion. "From what I remember about the man, he looked tall, and he was thin," Malang, now retired, recalls. "He was hanging half in and half out of the window of a small shack that was maybe eight feet wide by eight feet tall. Apparently, he died while attempting to crawl out of that window. I remember not moving the man because of the unusual position of his body, so I don't remember ever seeing his face."

If "Baltusrol Red" Kier and the "Red" of West Orange were one and the same, this person would have had to travel less than twelve miles to his new makeshift dwelling in the woods. Also of note, at least four golf courses are located within a three-mile range of the site where the body of West Orange "Red" was discovered. These golf clubs obviously would have provided ample caddying opportunities for this wanderer.

While Ed Cardinal does not have any recollection of "Baltusrol Red" Kier, he does remember another strange character who roamed the Houdaille Quarry. "There was this weird guy who worked at the quarry as a watchman. He was tall and skinny and wore glasses. I think he drove either an open jeep or a small motorcycle. I believe there was a gate to get into the quarry, but the fire department, police, road department and people that used the shooting range back in the far corner had a key or access to the key. If you went into the quarry, that guard would always show up."

"The guard's name was Tommy Rillo," says Ed Kisch. "He lived over in Summit. Tommy would have been anywhere from, say, twenty-eight to thirty-four years old at the time of the DePalma incident. He worked at the quarry, I think, because he was friends with the people that worked there

The Baltusrol Golf Club, pictured in 1926. *Courtesy of the Baltusrol Golf Club.*

from Summit. These were very friendly people up there. They all knew each other; they all got along good."

Peter Hammer also recalls the quarry's watchman. "Tommy was handicapped. He was fourteen years old in a thirty-year-old's body, but he was friendly with the police."

"Tommy was a little slow, mentally," Kisch continues. "I don't believe he was *impaired*, but he was just…That was a good job for him. His job was to watch the equipment and lock the gates at night. He had a pickup truck that he would ride around the quarry. He had a Detex clock that he carried. There were keys in various spots at the quarry, and he would stick the key into the Detex clock, and it would make a punch mark in the paper on the time. This way, the quarry could tell that he was doing rounds. Basically, he was there to keep people that weren't supposed to be in the quarry out."

Ed Kisch does not agree, however, with Ed Cardinal's recollection of one not being able to enter the quarry without this watchman immediately showing up. "Eddie Cardinal, for some reason, believes that nothing got past Rillo. I have to tell you, Tommy Rillo could be working up there, and you could ride around for a half hour, forty-five minutes to an hour before you could find Tommy. God knows where he was. He was in the quarry *someplace*. But we didn't go looking for him. He did his thing there. That was between him and the quarry. Me and other guys from the department used to go there all the time without Rillo seeing us. We used to set booby traps for him and shit."

Many in Springfield have long wondered how Tommy Rillo or any other Houdaille personnel never encountered Jeannette's body during the six

The Houdaille Construction Materials Company logo can be found on many pieces of abandoned equipment that still litter the area. *Photo by Jesse P. Pollack.*

weeks that it lay on top of the Devil's Teeth. According to Ed Kisch, Tommy Rillo never discovered the remains due to the fact that his duties involved guarding the various buildings inside of the quarry, and these duties would not have placed him in the area of that particular cliff top. "At the time that the body was found, I don't believe that there were any buildings over there at all," Kisch recalls. "Now, the only buildings that would have been on that side, maybe a hundred yards away from where the body was, were the buildings that some of the explosives were stored in. They would have been painted red. They were thick, heavy metal. They didn't really store the explosives there for any period of time because whenever they did what they called a 'shoot,' the quarry would drill holes according to the specifications of the company that would go to do the explosion. Then, they would bring the explosives up, they would lock them in the shed, they would take them out and they would put them in the holes. They would fill the holes, and then they would do their blast. So, as far as at the time, back in 1972, there were no buildings on the side of the quarry where Jeannette was found. That was an area that Rillo would not have checked. It was all trees. It was overgrown. There were no buildings over there that the quarry owned."

When asked if he believes that Tommy Rillo could have been responsible for Jeannette DePalma's death, Kisch answers in the negative. "I don't believe Tommy was ever even questioned," Kisch says. "That's not to say that somebody didn't question him, but I don't believe he ever was."

We were able to obtain the e-mail address of a Tom Rillo who currently lives not very far from Springfield. When we asked this man if he was the same Tommy Rillo who used to work as a watchman at the Houdaille Quarry, we received this cryptic reply: "No Jeanne… :)" We received no explanation for this confusing piece of correspondence.

Soon after the discovery of Jeannette's body, a few of Springfield's residents began to wonder if Jeannette had become the victim of a tragic accident due to certain police activity that often occurred inside the quarry gates. "The Springfield Police Department had a pistol range up in the quarry," Ed Kisch recalls. "We would use that for a lot of police training anytime we wanted to, and the Springfield Pistol and Rifle Club would basically use it on a Saturday or Sunday." Those in town who possessed knowledge of this makeshift pistol range began to quietly wonder if the supposed victim of witchcraft had actually been killed by a stray bullet, and the Springfield Police Department had covered up the death. Ed Kisch believes that this rumor is baseless simply on the grounds of the location of the range itself. "That range was totally on the other side of the quarry. If we say the body was found on the east side, the pistol range would be in the southwest corner of the quarry. In other words, they would have been shooting in the southeast direction. She would have been found in the northeast section of the quarry. So if you were to enter the quarry, you would turn to the right and drive along, go through the pits and come out the back to get to the pistol range. If you wanted to get to where was the body was, you would have driven into the quarry and over to the left."

The rumors regarding the Springfield Police Department's culpability in Jeannette's death did not end there. As time went on, a tale was slowly spun that pointed the finger at one of Chief George Parsell's sons. This particular piece of gossip eventually made its way to the DePalma family.

"What I had heard was that it had something to do with a chief of police at the time, his son," John Bancey said during his 2004 interview with *Weird NJ* magazine. "The theory that they had was, and I can't prove this, was that one of the police chiefs had a son who liked my aunt. She went to go to work, something happened, whatever it may be, and she ended up dead. I was told that he committed suicide a time later. I'm not sure; I can't verify this. That's what we thought had happened. We were told his son might have been the perpetrator, and he was so guilty—I was told he liked my aunt, but she had another boyfriend she went to the prom with. And he felt so guilty that he committed suicide. We believed that she was put in a place that somebody from the police department, or who knew the police department, would know because it was a high-up area, and it's not far from the police shooting range at the time. That's the old quarry. But we feel that maybe somebody placed a couple sticks around her to make it look like 'Hey, this is what happened.' But that's bullshit."

"I will guarantee you that rumor came from a cop," says Ed Kisch. "There were a significant number of cops that hated Parsell's guts because he was the chief of police, and these were the types of immature games that some of those cops played. One of Parsell's sons lived in California with his mother. He worked for an airline, and every now and then, Chief Parsell would call him up and ask him to get him tickets to fly to Florida in the spring. I don't know where the other son lived. He may have possibly lived in New Jersey, but he had no contact with his father. None whatsoever. That son did not get along with Chief Parsell."

We were able to verify that neither of Springfield police chief George Parsell's sons committed suicide shortly after the death of Jeannette DePalma. Stephen Parsell is still alive and living in California, and Gary Parsell died in New Jersey in 2002, three decades after his father's department first received the phone call about an arm found on Wilson Road. Another matter that makes this theory particularly dubious is the fact that Gary and Stephen were seven and nine years older than Jeannette, respectively, and would have had virtually no social interaction with her. This is highlighted by Kisch's recollection of Stephen already living and working in California at the time of Jeannette's disappearance and subsequent death.

Another possible origin of this rumor is the fact that Jeannette DePalma and Gail Donohue used to accept rides from the Summit and Springfield

Police while hitchhiking. "The cops knew me," Donohue recalls. "We usually got a ride by cop down to the train station."

All in all, Ed Kisch does not believe that the answers to the mysteries surrounding Jeannette DePalma's death lie with Red Kier, Tommy Rillo, the Parsells or any other publicly acknowledged person of interest in this case. In his heart, Kisch believes that the answers to these questions lie with a red Ford Falcon.

Around the time that Jeannette had gone missing, the Springfield Police Department received an alarm call from a home located in the Springfield Top neighborhood. Working the early morning patrol shift, Kisch was asked to respond to the call. "It was early in the morning, maybe around six thirty," Kisch recalls. "The sun was just coming up." Turning his police cruiser onto Mountview Road, the patrolman noticed something strange out of the corner of his eye—a car parked at the base of the hill leading to the Devil's Teeth cliff overlooking the Houdaille Quarry. "There was a red Ford Falcon parked in the area that would have been directly below where the body was later found. I remember thinking to myself, 'What the hell is that car doing in there?' but I kept on driving toward the house on top of Mountview Road. Had I not been on that alarm call, I would have been out of the car and where that Ford Falcon was. I went up to the house, checked it out and everything was fine. When I came back down Mountview Road, that Falcon was gone. No more than a half hour had gone by. Then, lo and behold, we find Jeannette's body on top of the cliff, that same cliff, about six weeks later."

When asked if Jeannette had any friends who drove a red Ford Falcon, Melissa Benner replied, "Cindy told me that a guy in a red or orange convertible used to pick her and Jeannette up when they hitchhiked."

"I don't think he drove a Falcon," Cindy DePalma says, "but this guy Mike used to pick us up. He was local, had dark hair and was a couple of years older than us. Maybe seventeen or eighteen." Today, Cindy DePalma cannot remember the exact make and model of this person's car, but she says that it closely resembled an early 1970s Chevrolet Camaro. "Mike liked Jeannette a lot," Cindy continues. "It made her uncomfortable." When asked if she feels that this person was capable of murdering her sister, Cindy replies briefly and to the point: "Yes." In conversation, Cindy describes this person as predatory and believes that, despite feeling uncomfortable around him, Jeannette may have accepted rides from him during the times she would hitchhike alone. Cindy DePalma says that she is unable to recall this person's last name.

In late June 2003, *Weird NJ* magazine received a letter from Rose MacNaughton,* a former resident of Springfield. In this letter, MacNaughton shed light on an individual whom she believes killed Jeannette DePalma—and this person bears more than a superficial resemblance to the predatory individual described by Cindy DePalma and Melissa Benner.

"I have given this much thought and believe I should divulge the name of the person I suspect," MacNaughton's letter reads. "As I told you in previous correspondence, I am not the only person who believes this person had something to do with Jeannette's murder. The person I suspect is Mike A. [We have chosen to withhold this man's entire name out of privacy concerns for his family.] He lived on Littlebrook Road, Springfield. He believed he was a warlock and told me personally he was a warlock. When Jeannette was a freshman at Jonathan Dayton High School, he was a junior or senior. There was something *very strange* about him. He was the type of person who made your hair stand on end. He liked Jeannette, but she did *not* return his affection. As I wrote previously, he moved abruptly. To where, I don't know."

We were eventually able to track down Rose MacNaughton over a decade after she sent her letter to *Weird NJ* magazine. Her recollections of Mike A. have not changed, and her belief in his guilt has not wavered.

"I would bet my bottom dollar that Mike A. is the one responsible for Jeannette's murder," she says. "I have been convinced of this for forty-two years, and I am not the only person who feels this way. People that you have already spoken with that are friends of mine feel this way. I know some of them would not speak to you because they did not want to get involved. I knew Jeannette through Cindy DePalma. Cindy and I are the same age, and we went to school together. Jeannette was a year ahead of us. We all went to grammar school at Our Lady of Lourdes in Mountainside. I was never really good friends with her, but I went to her house a few times. We used to hang out and play pool in their basement. I also knew Melissa Benner. Melissa and her sister went to Our Lady of Lourdes with us. I've known Melissa's sister since the fifth grade. I've known them very, very well for many, many years. Melissa knows full well who Mike A. is. Her sister knows full well who Mike A. is. Melissa knows—*and I know this for a fact*—that her sister and I believe that Mike A. was involved in this. Melissa probably does not want to dip her foot in this because she would have to bring her sister into it, and her sister does not want to deal with this in any way, shape or form. Jeannette would have very easily gotten into a car with Mike because she knew him."

MacNaughton reiterates that Mike A. lived on Littlebrook Road in Springfield, not far from Jeannette's home. Littlebrook Road also directly

Jeannette DePalma was last seen alive here at the corner of High Point Drive and Summit Road in Springfield—only two blocks away from a young man who was dangerously obsessed with the occult and had allegedly assaulted one of Jeannette's close friends. *Photo by Jesse P. Pollack.*

borders the Watchung Reservation, the supposed meeting grounds for witches, warlocks and devil worshippers. However, what is more notable and more disturbing is the fact that Mike A. lived only two blocks and a six-minute walk away from the corner of High Point Drive and Summit Road—the corner where Jeannette was last seen alive.

"The area where Jeannette would have been hitchhiking would have been on or around Summit Road," MacNaughton continues. "You have to go up Summit Road to get to Mike A.'s house."

MacNaughton, like Jeannette, also occasionally accepted rides from Mike A. in his 1971 Ford Torino 500—a muscle car that bears a noticeable resemblance to an early 1970s Chevrolet Camaro.

"He lived not far from where I lived, so he had given me a ride home from school a few times. He was a senior at Dayton when I was a freshman at Governor Livingston."

Just like the Mike Cindy DePalma remembers, Mike A. was eighteen years old at the time of Jeannette's death.

"At that time," MacNaughton continues, "Mike and the people he hung out with were very into witchcraft and those kinds of things. I wasn't into that at all. That was, pretty much, the beginning and end of any relationship that I was going to have with him. He was into things that I was brought up to believe are wrong. I was initially impressed with Mike because he was a senior and he had a car and long hair."

While MacNaughton cannot remember exactly when or where she and Mike A. initially met, she can, however, clearly recall when she became aware of his dark fascinations.

"The exact moment that I knew Mike was into witchcraft was one day when he and I were at my house in Mountainside. There was nothing sexual going on, but it got to the point where we were possibly going to kiss one another. At that time, I used to wear a diamond crucifix necklace. He looked at it and said, 'I can't come near you while you're wearing that.' Then I was 100 percent sure that this person was involved in things that I did not want to become involved in. That was the beginning and the end of that friendship. I remember that moment clearly. He was no longer a person that I wanted to be seen hanging out with or getting rides from."

During her interview with us, Rose MacNaughton discussed two individuals whom she believes participated in occult rituals with Mike A. MacNaughton also believes that these two people played a role in Jeannette's murder. We have chosen not to publish the names of these individuals but have notified investigators regarding these allegations.

According to MacNaughton, Mike A. quickly left Springfield shortly after the discovery of Jeannette DePalma's remains in September 1972. "Mike and his mother disappeared from the area!" she recalls. "Mike's father passed away either shortly before that or shortly after that, and he and his mother sold the house and moved away to, I think, New England."

During a June 2009 interview with Kevin Ranoldo, an independent researcher, Melissa Benner discussed her memories of Mike A. During these interviews, Benner claimed that Mike A. was "very aggressive" with many female students at Jonathan Dayton High School and had allegedly sexually assaulted some of them. Benner also claimed that Mike A. had attempted to rape her sometime in 1972, but she had managed to fight him off and escape. During these interviews, Benner also emphasized that Mike A. was strongly attracted to Jeannette and feared that her friend would become his next target. Melissa Benner reiterated these memories during several interviews with us.

If Mike A., an alleged "warlock" with sexually aggressive tendencies toward his female peers, was in fact responsible for the murder of Jeannette

DePalma, does this mean that the sensational headlines alluding to witchcraft and Satanism were actually not that far from the truth? Only one person knows for certain, and that person has been forever silenced by the grave. Mike A. died in 2010 at the age of fifty-six.

"Here's a twist regarding the telemarketing company that Jeannette and I worked for," says Gail Donohue. "I forget my co-worker's name, but she insisted that Jeannette called and said that she would be late for work on the day that she went missing. That was not told to me until four or five days after Jeannette's body had been found. In fact, this girl did not tell me this until after the shit hit the fan with the witchcraft rumors, and I talked to the detectives about the sensationalism in the newspapers. I went into work crying my eyes out. This one girl said, 'Well, that couldn't have happened. Don't you remember? Jeannette called in. They told you.' I said, 'She never told me anything!' Jeannette and I were supposed to go to work together that day after hanging out with the boys from Echo Lake Park. We would have hitchhiked down to the train station and taken the train."

Is it possible that Jeannette had run into a friend while hitchhiking—a friend who had much more enticing plans to offer her that day? Perhaps she was driven to a payphone in order to call out of work for the night. But if so, why did Jeannette not call her best friend to break their plans? Is it possible that Gail's co-worker was simply mistaken or, at the very least, incorrectly remembering the date of Jeannette's phone call? These questions, like so many others, may be forever left unanswered.

Gail Donohue is still convinced that Jeannette did not accept a ride from anyone she could have deemed a threat. "Jeannette was a toughie, but we all have an intuition about danger," she says. "At least I do. You know, the classic hair on the back of your neck standing up. If you're a hitchhiker, there is no way you're going to get into a car feeling that way."

Like countless others, Lisa Treich Greulich believes that Jeannette was, indeed, killed while hitchhiking. However, unlike Rose MacNaughton, Lisa does not believe that her cousin's murderer was driving a Ford Torino 500—or even a red Ford Falcon. "After Jeannette went missing, I had a premonition," Lisa says. "I was lying in bed, trying to fall asleep. All of a sudden, my body went limp. I couldn't move." Lisa claims that she then saw a clear vision of her cousin hitchhiking along Mountview Road. "It was like a dream, but I knew that I was awake. She was just standing there with her thumb out when this guy in a big green Buick pulled over. He was straight-laced. He didn't look like us hippies." Lisa remembers this man having a blond crew cut and wearing black horn-rimmed glasses.

"Jeannette seemed to be familiar with him," Lisa continues. "She got into his car, and I watched them pull off." What Lisa saw next caused her to experience a sensation of overwhelming dread. "The man parked his Buick at the base of a cliff in the woods. He and Jeannette both got out of the car at the same time and started walking toward this path in the woods near the cliff." Then, almost as soon as it began, the vision ceased. "As soon as it ended, I was able to move again. I ran into my mother and stepfather's room, screaming and crying. I tried to tell them what I had seen, but my mother didn't want to hear any of it. She insisted that I was simply having a nightmare, but my stepfather believed me. He tried to tell my mother to listen, but she wouldn't." Lisa received the shocking phone call the very next day: her cousin's body had been found lying on top of a cliff in the woods surrounding the Houdaille Quarry.

Unbeknownst to Lisa Treich Greulich, a seemingly straight-laced man who drove a green Buick would later be found at the center of another high-profile crime, one that was considered by many inside the Union County Prosecutor's Office to be related to the death of Jeannette DePalma.

"When the DePalma file hit my desk, I almost immediately saw a connection," says former assistant Union County prosecutor Michael J. Mitzner. "This case looked just like a homicide that we had over in South Orange—a young woman named Kramer."

7

THE MYSTERIOUS DEATH OF JOAN KRAMER

She would never change, but one day at the touch of a fingertip she would fall to dust.
—Simone de Beauvoir, The Mandarins

S itting in the living room of her French countryside home, Marjorie
Lange Sportes holds the 1966 yearbook for Kent Place, an all-girls
preparatory school located in Summit, New Jersey. Contained within the
book's pages are the only photographs that Marjorie possesses of a friend
lost long ago at the hands of a killer.

"Joan was a beautiful girl," Marjorie says, focusing on the portrait marked
"Joan Leslie Kramer." "However, one of her greatest charms was that she
seemed completely oblivious of this fact," she continues. "She would have
had to be blind not to be aware of her good looks, but she considered them as
just a fact of life and not an indicator of who she was or what she considered
important." Joan's senior portrait is a fitting counterpart to Marjorie's
musings. The photograph shows an attractive young woman gazing off into
the distance, a soft smile gracing her unblemished face.

Marjorie was a year ahead of Joan at Kent Place, but due to both
girls belonging to the school's French Club, the two were able to strike
up a friendship. "The meetings of these clubs were the only times where
different age groups were able to really mix," she says. "Joan had an upbeat
personality and loved people. She was very open and easy with them and
treated everyone as if they were a potential friend. I was a very shy social
clunker at the time, and I remember being struck by her friendliness and

naturalness. I've often wondered if this accepting attitude had something to do with her death. It's too bad that in all the newspaper articles about her death, she is always labeled a 'socialite,' which makes her sound as if she were a terrible snob. Nothing could be further from the truth. I suppose her parents were very well off and all that, but she certainly never went on about it. This in a school where the first question a fellow classmate asked me, when I was a newcomer in the eighth grade, was 'How many maids do you have?'"

At a mere eighteen years of age, Joan Kramer was already firmly establishing herself as a liberal feminist. A whole two years before the women's liberation movement would gain significant national attention through the apocryphal bra burnings of the 1968 Miss America Pageant, Joan had already forged an identity that did not always sit well with her teachers and peers at Kent Place.

"Joan approached me once in one of the school hallways and told me she'd like to talk to me," Molly Hammett Kronberg, a schoolmate of Joan's, recalls. "What she said was pretty wild. She said that she had recently broken into the office of either the headmistress, Miss Wolfe, or the assistant headmistress, Miss Wilcox, so she could look up the IQ scores of her fellow students. She had found mine, and it was very high. Therefore, she wanted to be my friend."

Deborah Kooperstein, a fellow classmate at Kent Place, has a very similar recollection of this event. "One day as we were walking back from the music building, Joan told me a secret. She had broken into Miss Wolfe's office or the high school head and found her 'file,' which was filled with negative and damaging reports about her. She was a gutsy girl and not intimidated. While there, she looked at mine, and mine was filled with similar reports! She said that the administration would hurt our chances of getting into the colleges we wanted. In my case, I didn't get into real college and ended up at a junior college."

Today, Kronberg can only look back and laugh at the bold nature of her friend. "I was shocked but somewhat admiring that she had had the nerve to do that. I was startled by her frankness, to say the least. I was tickled by her telling me almost immediately that her brother Orin had done the same thing, or at least something similar, while he was at Yale."

"Joan was very funny," Sonia Leonardo Baxter recalls. "She could crack us all up in class. She was full of life; what I would call a 'drama queen' in the absolute best sense of the word. She filled up any room she entered. One could not ignore her."

"Studying history, or English or French with Joan was never boring or passive," recalls her friend and classmate Judith Small. "She probed and tested, she mocked and she brooked bullshit not at all. If there was a difference between what we were supposed to learn and what she thought made sense, she called it out. She dug deep, and when she thought she had to, she took risks. When we studied for a mid-year world history exam covering the French and Russian revolutions, we decided that, because we were desperately short on time, each of us would master one revolution. As I remember, I chose the French but also, out of caution, made sure I knew the basics of the Russian. Joan dove deep into the Russian and never looked back. I remember my heart sinking for her, seated not far away, when I broke the seal on the exam booklet and read the big essay topic: 'Compare the Russian Revolution with the French Revolution.'"

Joan's friends and classmates remember her as being a true rarity not only for her confidence and progressive views but for her outward appearance as well.

"I remember that she sunbathed with an aluminum foil device around her neck that attracted the sun," Deborah Kooperstein recalls. "She had a deep tan as a result."

Molly Hammett Kronberg, too, recalls her classmate's physical appearance often standing out just as much as her personality. "I liked her exotic looks and manner. Joan was exotic for many reasons, one of which was because she was Jewish. There were very few Jews at Kent Place and not many more Catholics. It was a totally WASP school and, in those days, had no black or Hispanic students, though that has changed now. Joan was beautiful, with green eyes and light brown hair that had a sort of blond suffused through it. She wore big gold-hoop

Joan Kramer in 1966. *Courtesy of Marjorie Lange Sportes and Nia Eaton.*

gypsy earrings, unlike the discreet studs we wore in our ears. She was just fabulous."

Behind Joan's seemingly self-assured exterior, however, was a carefully kept secret: she was suffering from lupus, a life-threatening disease that causes antibodies to attack healthy tissue. By the time of her senior year at Kent Place, Joan's condition required her to ingest daily doses of cortisone pills.

"One thing we absolutely did not talk about was her blood disease, which I knew about but of which she never spoke," Marjorie Lange Sportes says. "At the time, I had no idea what the disease was, nor of its gravity. Having found out later what it was, I'm kind of amazed it was being kept under control so well. I knew a nineteen-year-old girl who died of this disease, and I always thought lupus was pretty much fatal. That's real luck, isn't it? She won her battle against lupus only to be slaughtered by some psychopathic creep later on…"

Six years after graduating Kent Place, Joan was working on her doctorate in English at Columbia University in New York City. At the time, she was romantically involved with Bernard Davidoff, a fellow Columbia student, and talk of marriage was in the air. On the night of Tuesday, August 15, 1972, the two found themselves entertaining nearly thirty guests in Joan's childhood home at 65 Crest Drive in South Orange, New Jersey. Her parents, Julian and Ruth, had decided to throw a summer party for friends of theirs, and the young couple had been invited to take part in the festivities. Clad in a low-cut, ankle-length orange and white cocktail dress, blue jacket and high heels, Joan was certainly a sight to be seen in her family's comfortable home. To the unsuspecting eye, all seemed to be well with the beautiful young student, but unbeknownst to the partygoers, there was tension brewing between Joan and Bernard.

At some point during the party, an argument ensued between the two lovers, and Joan quietly slipped out of the house undetected, making her way out of her family's neighborhood, which sat at the top of the large mountain on South Orange's west side. Her heels busily clacking on the asphalt street, a frustrated Joan began the mile and a half walk into the village's small downtown area.

Once on South Orange Avenue, Kramer turned left into a small alley behind Gruning's ice cream parlor. A phone booth sat at the rear of the alley. Dialing a friend in Manhattan, Joan began to discuss the fight between her and Bernard. Hearing that Joan was significantly distraught, her friend advised her to calm down and catch a cab home. Joan agreed and told her friend that she would hail a taxi and head straight back to Crest Drive. The

Above: The former Kramer home at 65 Crest Drive in South Orange. *Photo by Mark Moran.*

Right: Joan Kramer walked to the rear of this alley to telephone a friend after leaving her parents' home in the wake of an argument. *Photo by Jesse P. Pollack.*

twenty-four-year-old graduate student then phoned her parents and told her family that she was "on a deserted street in Newark" and would be taking a taxi home shortly. The reason for Joan's identification of South Orange as Newark during this telephone call has never been established.

Kramer then walked back out of the alley to the front of Gruning's and made a right toward the mountain. For reasons that today remain unknown, instead of flagging down a taxi, Joan Kramer approached a vehicle that was stopped at the traffic light situated at the corner of South Orange Avenue and Sloan Street. This intersection sat directly at the base of the mountain leading to her parents' home. Approaching the driver's side window of the vehicle, she asked the motorist for a ride home.

"Where do you live?"

"I live on top of the hill."

"Get in."

This would be the last time anyone saw Joan Leslie Kramer alive. It was 12:30 a.m. on Wednesday, August 16, 1972.

Two days after Joan had vanished, her parents began to receive a series of strange phone calls from a man claiming to have kidnapped their daughter. During the course of these calls, the unidentified man, who spoke with

The train trestle at the intersection of Sloan Street and South Orange Avenue in downtown South Orange. *Photo by Jesse P. Pollack.*

a husky voice in either a West Indian or African accent, made demands for a ransom of $20,000. If this amount was delivered, the man promised to set Joan free. Julian Kramer, the wealthy president of Suburban Foods Incorporated and the Tantleff Beef Company, agreed to the amount and asked the caller for proof that Joan was still alive and well. Kramer was very much aware of his daughter's medical condition and feared that she would not survive long without her medication. In response to Kramer's request, the caller stepped away from the phone, and a loud squeal was heard in the background. Convinced that the squeal came from his captive daughter, Julian Kramer made arrangements with the caller to have the ransom money dropped off at a secret location.

Much to Julian Kramer's surprise, the money was not picked up during the first two attempts to pay his daughter's supposed kidnapper. Each time, the mysterious caller would claim that he could not locate the $20,000 that Kramer had left for him and that if he did not receive the payment soon, he would shoot Joan. "The next call you will receive," the man said, "will be to tell you where you can find your daughter's body." A new meeting point was selected, and Kramer was told to be there at 9:00 p.m. on Sunday, August 20. Joan's older brother, Orin, who was standing nearby recording the phone call, decided to follow his father in his own car in a desperate attempt to catch his sister's kidnapper. That Sunday night, Julian Kramer exited his car and walked to the predetermined spot, a phone booth across from Newark's Weequahic Park. He stepped inside, and the phone immediately rang. Kramer picked up the receiver and heard the supposed kidnapper at the other end. "I'm watching you," he said. Kramer then set the ransom money on the floor of the booth and walked back to his car. Orin Kramer raced to the phone booth but did not make it in time—the $20,000 vanished from the drop-off point nearly as soon as it arrived there.

Sadly, Julian Kramer had just handed away a large sum of money to an imposter. The fifty-three-year-old executive would later learn that a "senior South Orange homicide detective" had taken the cash from the phone booth. Experts listened to Orin Kramer's tapes of the ransom calls and determined that the foreign accent used by the caller was "phony." The man who had been harassing Kramer for the last several days had not kidnapped his daughter, nor was she being held hostage by any such kidnapper.

In reality, Joan Kramer had been dead the whole time.

On Monday, August 28, 1972, the nude body of Joan Leslie Kramer was found lying facedown inside of Union's Elizabeth River Park, only seven miles away from her parents' home. At the time, this secluded, wooded area just off Salem Road was located behind several stores and factories and was not easily accessible by an automobile. Unlike the Houdaille Quarry, where Jeannette DePalma's body would be discovered three weeks later, this area was never alleged to be a party spot or lover's lane. Seventeen-year-old John Hasenauer and a friend discovered Joan's swollen and discolored body sometime around 12:30 p.m. on that Monday while walking along a footpath near the Elizabeth River. The discovery almost did not occur, as Joan's decomposing remains were obscured by several bushes located in that particular area. Once the Union County Park Police were notified, Detective Sergeant Richard Mannix raced to the scene in order to secure the area and interview Hasenauer and his friend. Searching the area around Joan's body, Mannix discovered a three-foot-long piece of rubber hose within an arm's length of the remains and, later, a pickaxe nearly one hundred feet away. While it was later determined by the New Jersey State Police's crime lab that the piece of hose had nothing to do with Joan's murder, the pickaxe was eventually determined to have been used in an attempt to bury Joan's clothing, which was turned over to the police a day after her body was recovered. Joan's orange and white dress, along with the blue suede jacket that she had been seen wearing last, were located in a grassy area across the street from the site of her remains by Nathaniel Fennell, a Union County Park Commission attendant. Fennell had found the discarded articles of clothing tangled in weeds near the banks of the river four days prior. It was also later discovered that Kramer's wallet had been found in the Elizabeth River by three teenagers only one day after the young woman had disappeared. The youths did not report this discovery until after Kramer's body was found. Two items, however, were not recovered. Joan's shoes were missing, and like Jeannette DePalma, a necklace that she had been wearing was never found.

After Joan Kramer's body was removed from Elizabeth River Park during the afternoon of August 28, 1972, an autopsy was immediately conducted by Essex County medical examiner Dr. Edwin A. Albano. Due to the extent of decomposition, Dr. Albano relied on dental records to make a positive identification. The knowledge of two preexisting scars on Joan's body also aided the identification process. During his examination, Albano found no antemortem bruising on the body, but he did locate a large pressure mark on Joan's throat. This pressure mark led Albano to dissect the neck in order to search for a possible cause of death. During the dissection, Albano discovered that a neck bone had been fractured, leading to the collapse of Joan's windpipe. The immediate result of this was asphyxiation, which ultimately

Joan Kramer's body remained undetected in this secluded location, just off Salem Road in Union, for nearly half a month. *Photo by Jesse P. Pollack.*

killed Joan Kramer. Further analysis aided Dr. Albano in determining that Joan had been murdered via manual strangulation, which was administered by a right-handed individual who was standing either in front of or to the left of her. In his report, Albano noted that Kramer had been dead for at least a week to ten days and that he would not be able to determine whether she had been sexually assaulted without the aid of additional testing.

If Jeannette DePalma died due to strangulation, as per Dr. Bernard Ehrenberg's assumption, that would mean that both she and Joan Kramer were murdered in the exact same way. This would not be the only obvious similarity. Both Joan and Jeannette were young, attractive women of average height and weight with long, straight, brunette hair that was worn with a part in the middle. Both women vanished within eight days of each other while allegedly hitchhiking, and both were later discovered dead, lying facedown in remote wooded areas only six miles apart. In both cases, necklaces were missing from the bodies.

These similarities were not lost on the Union County Prosecutor's Office. After both cases were examined by investigators, the decision was made to utilize a telephone tip line exclusively dedicated to both the Kramer and DePalma cases. Assistant prosecutor Michael Mitzner told reporters that the

The final resting place of Joan Kramer. *Photo by Jesse P. Pollack.*

"special police telephone number of 352-5300" had been set up to "receive information on the death of either girl."

No tip or clue of any worth ended up being called in.

On Tuesday, August 29, 1972, following a simple ceremony held at the Temple B'nai Jeshurun in Short Hills, the body of Joan Kramer was driven by hearse to the B'Nai Abraham Memorial Park in Union, where it was laid to rest beneath the shade of a large tree. "I remember vividly the sobs of Mrs. Kramer as Joan's coffin was lowered into the waiting grave," says Molly Hammett Kronberg. "She broke down completely. It was one of the most harrowing sounds I have ever heard."

"It was hard when she died," Sonia Leonardow Baxter says. "The first piece of our innocence died. We all mourned her. She held such promise."

Judith Small is still hit very hard by the death of her friend. "Joan was the first to leave us, and because someone took her deliberately, her loss will always seem the most cruel," she says. An accomplished poet, Small later channeled her profound grief into a poem that appeared in a 1976 issue of *New Letters* magazine. The piece, simply titled "Poem for Joan," reads:

I do not want
to know what you were thinking the night
you disappeared.

Already I know too much:

the flickering light of a television
all afternoon
                        the wrists
of an old man in pajamas watching,
shuffling a deck, reshuffling
                                or in Spain last week
a child shifting
its weight in the womb,
the mother at the last minute pardoned, permitted
to live out her life in prison.

Always the exquisite
cowardice of the intellect,
pressing a tailored suit before
appointments with suffering.
                            There is
enough suffering.

From the vacant lot where your body was found, the smell
of cucumbers turning soft.
                        The moon's skin
has an unhealthy sheen at the edge of
Newark, late in August.
I know now:
every driver on the freeway is a lunatic with teeth
invisible
as cucumber seeds.

I am frightened, Joan, and I want
to live bravely.
                For grandfathers,
children, skylarks this
is a stinking country.
                    Sing to me
with a crow's voice,
without loveliness, fiercely

earthbound.

"The poem has always been very important to me," Small says, "as a kind of anchor, I think, as well as a way of trying to come to terms with the loss of Joan. I was able to send it to Joan's mother, Ruth, after it was published, and she sent me a very warm note in response, which, of course, meant the world to me. I almost always include the poem when I give readings. In fact, I often start with it and have always felt a strong response from audiences. Long ago, Ruth Kramer came to a reading I gave in New Jersey, so I was able to read the poem aloud to her as well. Over the years, the poem has become a way for me to keep the memory of Joan's spirit alive and to share it with others. It has also given me a way to return, again and again, to the courage that, for me, defined her."

Only hours after Joan Kramer's burial, the former List home at 431 Hillside Avenue in Westfield mysteriously caught fire. Rumors began to swirl about arson. First responders claimed to have smelled kerosene while fighting the fire. Others accused the Westfield Police Department of secretly torching the house of horrors to stop Breeze Knoll from quickly becoming a grim tourist attraction. Others who were close to the List investigation told reporters that a group of teenagers who were engaged in a séance had

The former List home at 431 Hillside Avenue in Westfield. This photo was taken the morning after the bodies of John List's family were found lying on sleeping bags in the ballroom. The house mysteriously burned to the ground nine months later, in August 1972. *Collection of the authors.*

accidentally knocked over a candle, setting the abandoned home ablaze. Today, the cause of the fire is still undetermined.

As the Kramer family grieved, the South Orange Police Department continued to investigate Joan's brutal murder. The Essex County Park Police began a series of foot searches inside of the South Mountain Reservation, while detectives from the Union County Park Police interviewed several residents of the Putnam Manor section of Union who claimed to have heard a woman screaming as she fled from a car around the time of the murder. This neighborhood sits less than one mile away from the area where Joan's body was later recovered. Investigators also began to look into eyewitness reports of a young woman entering a car stopped at the intersection of South Orange Avenue and Sloan Street on the night Joan vanished. One such witness, a fifty-year-old widow named Mary Colato, met with Sergeant George Homa of the South Orange Police Department. Over the course of a three-hour session, Colato was able to provide enough information about the driver of the vehicle for Homa to create a composite sketch. Shortly thereafter, the department released this new sketch of their prime suspect to the news media. Local newspapers carried the sketch in their continuing coverage of the Kramer case.

One South Orange family recognized the man in the sketch as not just someone they casually knew but as their very own neighbor.

8

THE ACCOUNTANT

Where's evil? It's that large part of every man that wants to hate without limit, that wants to hate with God on its side. It's that part of every man that finds all kinds of ugliness so attractive.
—*Kurt Vonnegut,* Mother Night

T hat house was *possessed*. There was something evil in that house."
Curt Knoth is haunted by the memories of his neighbors. Growing up in the suburban village of South Orange, Knoth can clearly remember the point in his childhood where innocence was not just lost but shattered. It all began when he saw a familiar face in the local newspaper: "When that witness sketch from the Kramer case appeared in the newspaper, everyone in South Orange knew right away that it was Otto Nilson…"

Otto Neil Nilson was born on October 13, 1934, in New York to Otto N. Nilson III and Helen Nilson. A graduate of Seton Hall University, Nilson served in the United States military and later married Carole S. Spangenberger. The couple had five children and chose to settle down in a home on Summit Avenue in South Orange. Otto supported his large family by working at an accounting firm while Carole took care of their children at home.

During their initial years in South Orange, the Nilsons were a popular and well-liked family who fit in well with the tightknit community. "Mr. Nilson was a very big guy and very sweet," recalls Alex Mason,* a former neighbor. "If he came to our yard when the kids were playing ball, he would throw the ball around with them for a few minutes."

"People liked the Nilsons, and everyone got along," Curt's sister, Audrey Knoth Muratore, recalls. "He was a nice guy. When we were little and had loose teeth, my mother would say, 'Go over and see Mr. Nilson; he'll take it out for you.' Mr. Nilson was good at taking teeth out. We would always go over there when we had loose teeth."

Curt Knoth has similar recollections. "We used to have these huge barbecues, and all the parents would sit around in a circle and drink all night long," he says. "Everyone was always very excited to see Mr. Nilson come over the house. This was the whole World War II generation, and Otto was military, so there was appreciation for that. He was hilarious and had this really magnificent personality. Everyone would talk to him. I remember him throwing us around on his back. He looked like Clark Kent. At these barbecues, he was like the grand master of ceremonies."

However, this would soon change.

"Around 1970 or so, Otto went bad," Knoth says. During this period of time, Otto and Carole began to drink heavily. As a result, their children and home went neglected. "The house was actually shut down, or condemned or whatever you might call that," Knoth continues. "All of the Nilson kids had to go to the hospital to get de-flead and have their hair cut and shampooed. It was disgusting. I mean, they would leave dirty dishes out on the table forever and just throw them away and use paper plates. I mean, it was *bad*. It was gross."

"Mrs. Nilson was an alcoholic," says Audrey Knoth Muratore. "She finally recovered after many years, but when you're drinking like that, you just don't get your shit together."

Soon after, the Nilsons' problems began to extend to their neighbors.

"There was an incident where my father went to a party and the Nilsons were there," Audrey Knoth Muratore recalls. "Otto left, and my dad and this other guy had to drive Carole home. Otto met them on the front porch in his underwear. He was in kind of a rage. Now, my dad is about five-six and slim, and this other guy was only five-three. Mr. Nilson was a pretty big guy, and let's just say that they knew if any fight was going to happen, they were going to lose. It was one of those scary situations."

As his drinking worsened, Otto Neil Nilson became violent toward his family. "My best friend at that time was Nilson's son Neil," Knoth says. "One day in 1970 or '71, we were playing with Hot Wheels in Neil's room, and we heard a commotion upstairs in the attic where Mr. Nilson was working. We heard a big bang—a crash. Neil ran right upstairs. Mr. Nilson was there, and he had cut his hand. He had blood all over his hand. He looked very, very strange. I mean, he looked cuckoo. He screamed, '*GET THE FUCK OUT*

OF HERE!" and we went right back down the steps." Something else about this incident disturbed the young Curt Knoth. "When we were downstairs, we heard voices up there. It sounded like somebody else was up there with Mr. Nilson, but he was *alone*."

Carole Nilson began telling friends and neighbors that her husband had grown cold toward her and that the two were fighting more and more often. Eventually, she asked Otto to leave and filed for divorce. "Mrs. Nilson had some kind of restraining order, and Mr. Nilson wasn't allowed back there. Of course, he would go back there once in a while, and there would be a big problem or hassle."

One of these hassles stands out very clearly in Knoth's memory.

"Sometime around 1972, Otto showed up at Carole's house," he says. "I think he might have smacked her around, and she called the police. My mother was right in the middle of that. We heard the sirens and saw Nilson's daughter walking up to our house with her baby brother. She handed him to my mother. Neil and I walked down to his house, and Mr. Nilson came out the front door. South Orange and Maplewood Police drove up from both sides, and a fight ensued on the front steps. I mean, Mr. Nilson was a *big* guy. He took three cops and just threw them away. They took a clothesline from our neighbor's house and tied him up with it. Mr. Nilson smacked Mrs. Nilson around more than one time. No doubt about that."

By this time, Nilson had moved out of town to live with his mother. The village of South Orange, however, was not about to forget the thirty-seven-year-old accountant. A familiar-looking sketch that would appear in the local newspapers in August of that year would see to that.

"There was a witness sketch made of the person who picked up Joan Kramer in South Orange Village," Curt Knoth recalls. "It appeared in the *Star-Ledger*, I think. I remember my mother looking at it and saying, 'It's Mr. Nilson.' She said, 'That's him.'"

Audrey Knoth Muratore also remembers the witness sketch. "When that picture was in the newspaper that summer, I can remember saying to my mother, 'Hey! That picture looks like Mr. Nilson!' and my mother saying, 'No, no, no! That's not him! What are you talking about?' But later on, I overheard her talking to her friends, saying, 'Even Audrey thinks it looks like him.' After that happened, my mother told me to stay away from Mr. Nilson and that if I saw him, to go the opposite way."

Mrs. Knoth's mind immediately turned to another young woman who had been murdered only a mile and a half away nearly six years prior—a young woman whose killer had never been found.

On the evening of Thursday, November 3, 1966, the body of seventeen-year-old Carol Ann Farino was found lying in a driveway on Sommer Avenue in Maplewood. She had been strangled with her own stocking. Maplewood patrol officer Anthony M. Surano Jr. tried in vain to save Carol Ann's life by administering mouth-to-mouth resuscitation after Officers James O'Dowd and James Waddell quickly cut the silk stocking from her throat. At 9:05 p.m., twenty-one minutes after the discovery of her body, Carol Ann Farino was pronounced dead at the scene by Dr. J. Evans. Carol Ann's body was then turned over to the local morgue.

Just like Joan Kramer, Carol Ann Farino's shoes were never recovered. Just like Jeannette DePalma, Carol Ann Farino's body was found across the street from a golf course.

If it is true that Jeannette did, indeed, die as the result of strangulation, all three women were killed the same way.

"I remember my mother and Mrs. Nilson talking about Carol Farino in my kitchen," Curt Knoth says. "They both wondered where Mr. Nilson was at the time that this girl was murdered. It was that kind of conversation. A pretty intense conversation, too. You know, Mrs. Nilson was putting it together in her head that maybe he was killing other people."

"My mom and Mrs. Nilson were very good friends," Audrey Knoth Muratore recalls. "Mrs. Nilson was over my house every single day with my mother, having coffee. I can tell you that right after Joan Kramer was murdered, they were talking about him being the one."

Billy Gregg, one of Nilson's former neighbors on Summit Avenue, also recalls the rumors surrounding the accountant's possible role in Farino's death. "Before the Kramer murder happened," Gregg says, "I vaguely remember either my mother or father telling me that Mrs. Nilson told one of them, or someone else that repeated it, that Mr. Nilson said something like, 'What a shame about that girl that was strangled coming home' before it was even reported." Billy Gregg recalls hearing that the young woman had been returning home from a Catechism class on the night of her murder. Furthermore, Gregg remembers Otto Neil Nilson teaching Catechism classes at Our Lady of Sorrows Roman Catholic Church in South Orange. We were unable to determine whether Carol Farino was a student of Nilson's, but according to a police report provided by the Maplewood Police Department, Farino had last been seen alive at George's Restaurant on Maplewood Avenue on the night of her death.

"Several months later, Mr. Nilson showed up at our door," Curt Knoth continues. "I was upstairs with my father at the time. At some point during my mother and Mr. Nilson's conversation, it turned into an aggressive thing. It was a commotion, more or less. All I heard were voices and him saying something loud. Maybe he thought that my mother was telling the police what was going on, or Mrs. Nilson said something about the conversations that they were having about him killing other girls. I don't know. I remember the South Orange Police being outside when he came into our house. They were following him. They knew something was going on. He was not our neighbor anymore, at this point. When I heard their conversation turn into an aggressive thing, I came down the steps, and about that time was when Mr. Nilson turned around and went back outside. I remember going up to the door, looking outside, and there were police there. There was a cop right in front of my house."

Audrey Knoth Muratore also recalls this incident but insists that there was no police involvement. "He wasn't arrested the night that he came to our house," she says. "My mother just got him out, *thank God*. She told us that things got uncomfortable. He was saying things like, 'Nobody loves me. I don't know what I'm going to do. I'm losing my family. I'm in a bad way,' and that kind of stuff. She was frightened. She just said, 'It's OK, don't worry about it. Everything is going to be fine,' and she just kept backing away from him. Not that he was making any sexual advances or anything, but he just kept coming closer to her. She basically just talked him off of the cliff, which was all that she could do, and he left on his own volition."

Carole Nilson was not the only resident of 410 Summit Avenue who was beginning to suspect that her ex-husband was a killer. "When I was about ten or eleven years old, Neil Nilson and I went down to Mr. Nilson's office in Maplewood," Curt Knoth recalls. "Neil was upset about something. He was going to confront his father with something. I could tell. I asked him what was bothering him, and Neil told me, '*I think my dad killed someone.*' We walked down to his office in Maplewood Village. It was on the top floor of a building. Neil was upstairs, and I was downstairs. A commotion happened. I ran up the stairs, and Mr. Nilson had his knee on Neil's chest and his hands around his throat. He yelled at us both to get out of the office, and we did the same thing as the last time; we ran out and we ran home. Neil was heartbroken. He was ruined."

"There were a lot of incidents with him during that period of time," Audrey Knoth Muratore recalls. "There was the night where things got crazy after my father dropped off Mrs. Nilson, and then there was the night that he went to the neighbors' house…"

In the early morning hours of July 7, 1974, the rage that seethed inside Otto Neil Nilson finally boiled over. Exiting his three-room apartment at 173

Maplewood Avenue, Nilson started the engine of his blue Buick and drove a mile and a half to his former home on Summit Avenue in South Orange. Looking to confront his ex-wife, Nilson smashed the front window of Carole Spangenberger's house and broke in. Manically dashing from room to room, Nilson soon discovered that his ex-wife and five children were nowhere to be found. Staring at a framed photograph of one of his sons, taken while the child was crying, Nilson lost whatever remaining composure he may have had. Darting across the street, he managed to convince himself that his former neighbors, the Gregg family, were somehow responsible for his family's absence. Carole Nilson often played poker with the Greggs, but in reality, the former Mrs. Nilson and her children were vacationing in Barnegat that weekend.

Just as the clock struck 2:00 a.m., Otto kicked in the front door of 415 Summit Avenue, destroying the door frame in the process. The resulting noise immediately woke forty-eight-year-old William Gregg from his slumber.

"I remember hearing the door break open, but I did not fully wake up," William's son Daniel recalls. "The front door was warped and often required a couple of hip-checks to open."

"That night, I had fallen asleep in the TV room after watching *Don Kirshner's Rock Concert*," Billy Gregg says. "I jumped up when Nilson blasted through the front door and found him standing in the living room. He said, 'Where's your father?' At that point, my father showed up on the stairway landing, and I said, 'Neil wants to see you.'"

Brushing past the nineteen-year-old Billy, Nilson raced up the stairs to confront the confused teenager's father with a forceful punch to the mouth. The blow busted William Gregg's lower lip open and launched him backward into a wall.

"I ran up the stairs and jumped on Nilson's back," Billy Gregg continues, "and we all went backward down the stairs. I cut my elbow on the railing as we went down."

"This was all in a matter of seconds," Daniel Gregg says. "I jumped out of bed and saw this tussle. In my grogginess, I thought it was my dad and brother fighting, even though nothing like that had ever happened in my house. Thinking it was my brother, I grabbed the head of the bottom guy to pull them apart but soon realized that this huge, whiskery head wasn't him and let go." The Greggs' struggle to subdue their nocturnal assailant then carried over into the living room.

Eventually, Billy Gregg was able to gain the upper hand and knocked Nilson to the floor. "My brother was a wrestler," Daniel Gregg recalls. "He put Nilson in a choke hold while my father tried to smash his knees with his heavy briefcase. He was kicking wildly while my brother restrained him by the neck."

"He tried kicking my old man," Billy Gregg says. "That's when I choked him and starting punching him in the forehead."

"My mom was screaming to the police on the phone while holding an iron by the cord," Daniel Gregg continues. "She was trying to bounce it on Nilson's head."

As Officers Bottona and Hahne of the South Orange Police Department entered the home, they found Billy Gregg still lying under Nilson, restraining him with a chokehold. "The cops came pretty quickly and pulled him up," Daniel Gregg says. "He seemed to settle for a second but then had a quick violent outburst. He picked up the end table and swung it at somebody. That end table somehow ended up on our front lawn. We never figured that one out…"

Bottona and Hahne were able to subdue Nilson before any further damage could be done to the home or its residents and immediately placed him under arrest. As their intruder was placed into a squad car, William Gregg and his wife were taken by ambulance to Orange Memorial Hospital to be treated for their injuries. "My brother drove the two of us to the hospital because we were too cool to take the ambulance," Daniel Gregg says with a laugh.

While being booked at South Orange Police Headquarters, Otto Neil Nilson provided no adequate explanation for his actions. Officer Robert Bottona would later describe Nilson's mindset as "irrational" while filing his incident report. As Nilson was being processed, Detective Lieutenant Sal Bollaro, along with Detectives Anthony Fabrizio and Gilbert Scott, immediately noticed a striking similarity between the cuffed accountant and a composite sketch that had been sitting in the South Orange Police Department's cold case files for nearly two years. All three policemen agreed that the man in front of them looked identical to the person who had allegedly picked up Joan Kramer on the night she was killed. An investigation into Otto Neil Nilson quietly began within the walls of South Orange's Detective Bureau.

This violent and unprovoked incident would haunt the Gregg family for years to come. "We moved out of our house largely because of that incident," Daniel Gregg says. "My mom kept seeing, or at least *thought* she was seeing, Nilson driving by, even though he had some kind of restraining order. It freaked her out, and she would put a chair in front of the door every night. It didn't help that my father traveled for work. I also remember that a murder similar to Joan Kramer's later happened, and police cars from

Otto Neil Nilson once resided in the small, three-room apartment on the second floor of this building at 173 Maplewood Avenue. *Photo by Mark Moran.*

that place, which might have been Bergen County, were at his house. I don't think anything came of it, though. After we moved away, we'd occasionally hear or read something bad about him. It's all a very sad story. He seemed like a really good guy to me before the divorce. He was active in the church, had a nice wife and five good kids."

After speaking with detectives and an Essex County judge, Nilson was charged with assault and ordered to undergo a fifteen-day psychiatric evaluation at Cedar Grove's Overbrook Asylum. After his evaluation was completed, Nilson received a two-year suspended sentence and was ordered to stay out of South Orange and away from his ex-wife. Nilson agreed to the terms and returned to his small Maplewood apartment.

"We went to Nilson's hearing for our break-in," Daniel Gregg recalls. "The judge said he was free to go, and my father got up in the courtroom to protest but was rebuked. He was later called aside, and someone explained to him that when the police arrested Nilson, he was recognized as a suspect for another crime, and they had to let him go until they got the evidence they needed."

Mere days after Otto Neil Nilson's release from Overbrook Asylum, the nearby township of North Bergen would be rocked to its core by the disappearance and subsequent murder of two teenage girls.

9

THE BERGEN GIRLS

Into the darkness they go, the wise and the lovely.
—Edna St. Vincent Millay, *"Dirge without Music"*

S he should have been home by now…"

The words danced around inside Wanda Pryor's mind, mercilessly taunting her, as she paced around her small North Bergen apartment. Pryor's daughter, seventeen-year-old Mary Ann, had left home around four o'clock that day. She had received a Macy's gift certificate for her birthday the month before and wanted to buy a few things for a planned trip to her aunt and uncle's home in Ortley Beach the next day. With the Garden State Plaza Mall in Paramus being only a short bus ride away, Mary Ann picked up the phone and called her friend, sixteen-year-old Lorraine Marie Kelly. Normally, Mary Ann would have asked her best friend, Diane Siebert, to join her on her shopping trip, but Diane was out of town on vacation that week. Lorraine agreed to join her friend and said she would be over shortly. It was now five hours later, and both girls had not arrived home, nor had either of their families heard from them.

Suddenly, Wanda Pryor's anxiety was lifted as she heard the front door of the apartment begin to open. Turning hear head toward the door, her heart began to race as her eldest daughter, nineteen-year-old Nancy, walked in instead of Mary Ann.

"Where is your sister?" Wanda asked.

"What are you talking about?" Nancy replied, visibly confused by her mother's inquiry. Nancy had seen her younger sister earlier that day and knew she had left to go to the mall with Lorraine, but surely she must be home by now.

"Your sister didn't come home," Wanda continued. "I've called everyone, and nobody knows where she is."

An undeniable feeling of apprehension now began to overwhelm Nancy. Mary Ann had told her that she would be home around 5:00 p.m. It was now well after 9:00 p.m.

"That was not like her," Nancy Pryor says. "If she was going to be late, she would have called. We contacted the police, but they said we had to wait twenty-four hours before filing a missing person report."

Not content to sit around waiting for too long, Nancy Pryor decided to hit the streets the next morning to search for her missing sister. "By dawn, it was apparent that she wasn't coming home," Nancy recalls. "I went out to look for Mary Ann while my parents stayed home and manned the phones. I went up to the bus stop, and then I went by Lorraine's house." Lorraine's older siblings, twenty-three-year-old Thomas and twenty-one-year-old Maureen, told Nancy that they had not seen or heard from their younger sister either. "I went all over the place," Nancy continues. "I asked Mary Ann's friends, and nobody saw her. It became like that for the next few days—no sleep, just worrying. Then, when we were finally able to file the report, the police insisted that they were just runaways. They were like, 'Oh yeah, she ran away from home.' We said, 'No, that's not like her.' She had no reason to run away from home. She was happy. She was going down the shore the next day. There was no reason, but the cops kept insisting that she was a runaway. I don't think the police did anything to try and find them, to be honest."

As Nancy Pryor continued to search for Mary Ann and Lorraine throughout North Bergen, her parents continued to receive the runaround from the North Bergen Police Department. "They really weren't keeping us posted," Nancy says. "We would get occasional calls. Of course, we kept calling them, and each time, they would just say, 'Yeah, we're working on it, but we have no leads.' The detectives felt that if they told us anything, it would ruin their investigation. They were afraid that we would say something to friends, family or reporters. They really didn't want us talking to reporters. We were mostly kept in the dark."

Once detectives became aware of Mary Ann's long-distance relationship with a young man in Georgia, the investigation was immediately focused on her boyfriend, Sal Rubiano.

"Somebody called me up and asked me if it was possible that Mary Ann had run away," Rubiano recalls. "They wanted me to let them know if Mary

Ann was coming down to Georgia to see me. I told them I would let them know. I started to get nervous, but it didn't make any sense [at] that time to think that anything bad had happened. If she was going to do something like that, I would have known she was coming on down. I knew nothing like that was happening because that's not something she would have done. Our relationship was a long-distance thing. We would communicate with each other by phone. Long-distance phone calls were very expensive back in those days, but sometimes I would use my dad's office phone to give Mary Ann a call. I wanted her to move down here with me, but she wanted to finish school first. She said her mother would kill her if she didn't finish high school. That was a bit of a letdown."

Once it became apparent that Mary Ann Pryor was not on her way to see Rubiano in Georgia, detectives from the North Bergen Police Department began to take a close look at Lorraine's boyfriend, seventeen-year-old Ricky Molinaro. Ricky had been the last person to see the girls on Friday, August 9, 1974. Molinaro had given Mary Ann and Lorraine a ride to a bus stop at the corner of Slocum Avenue and Broad Avenue in nearby Ridgefield that day and watched them board the 4:30 p.m. bus to the Garden State Plaza Mall. Molinaro claimed that he did not see Mary Ann or Lorraine after that, despite a prior arrangement with Lorraine to pick her up at Nungessers, a popular intersection on the Bergen/Hudson County line, at 9:00 p.m. that night. Lorraine, Ricky said, never showed.

When we asked him for an interview for this book, Ricky Molinaro replied, "I don't feel comfortable sharing personal things over a phone or e-mail. Sorry, can't help."

While the North Bergen Police Department questioned potential witnesses and issued a thirteen-state missing person alert for the teenage girls, the families of Mary Ann and Lorraine helplessly awaited any piece of information. The suspense began to take its toll on Wanda Pryor, who began to fear the worst. "I feel like they're in the bushes some place," she told a reporter from the *New York Daily News*.

On Tuesday, August 13, the Pryor and Kelly families received a hopeful piece of news. A waitress at the Couch House Diner in Union City told the North Bergen Police Department that she had witnessed two teenage girls matching the descriptions of Mary Ann and Lorraine dining at the establishment around five thirty that morning. Investigators felt that this tip held particular merit, as the waitress was able to accurately describe clothing similar to that which Mary Ann and Lorraine were last seen wearing. The North Bergen Police Department then went to the press and declared the girls to be runaways, with Lieutenant James Braddock announcing, "There is no longer any reason to fear that the girls are victims of foul play." Braddock would regret this statement in a matter of hours.

The very next day, on the morning of August 14, 1974, a tenant of Ridgemount Gardens apartment complex in Montvale would make a horrific discovery. Exiting the building's front door, fifty-nine-year-old Enis Perry made her way over to her car, which was parked in the adjacent lot. Opening the driver's side door, she noticed something peculiar out of the corner of her eye. In a sloping, wooded area only ten feet from the bumper of Perry's car were two nude bodies, lying facedown and parallel to each other. The bodies were badly discolored, and each had a rope loosely tied around the neck. Most shocking of all, each girl had a glass soft drink bottle inserted into her vaginal cavity. Perry immediately raced back inside her apartment and phoned the police. Officer Carl Olsen of the Montvale Police Department was the first to arrive at the crime scene, and the patrolman quickly secured the area. Olsen observed a noticeable lack of blood on and around the bodies, leading him to believe that the two had been killed elsewhere.

"The bodies seem to have been placed—and I mean placed, not thrown," Montvale police commissioner Thomas Maurer later told the *New York Times*. "It was a horrible scene. The bodies looked like two little dolls at Christmastime…" Marks found around the girls' wrists and ankles indicated that they had been tied up before their murder, the ropes around their necks having possibly been used to hogtie the teenagers. As investigators combed the area for evidence, it soon became apparent that the two girls had been dumped without their clothing, shoes or pocketbooks. The only personal effects that appeared to have been left untouched by the killer were a necklace and a bracelet found on one of the bodies and a necklace found on the other. Montvale detectives got their first clue once they took a close look at Lorraine's necklace: a gold chain with a pendant that read, "Lorraine and Ricky." As investigators from the Bergen County Prosecutor's Office made plaster casts of footprints found near the bodies, Montvale's homicide detectives made contact with the North Bergen Police Department. Once the department was alerted to a possible match between the yet-to-be-identified bodies and the two missing teenagers, North Bergen detective Vincent DeCarlo raced to the Pryors' apartment on Second Avenue. The forty-five-year-old detective hoped to reach Mary Ann's family before the press did. Unfortunately, his attempt would be in vain.

"We heard it on the radio," Nancy Pryor recalls. "We had that news station, 1010 WINS, on constantly. About five minutes later, they knocked on the door." Detective DeCarlo was let into the Pryors' apartment by a family friend. Nancy had been keeping vigil by the telephone while her father, James, paced around the apartment and her mother chain-smoked cigarettes, all hoping to be told that the bodies found in Montvale were not those of Mary Ann and Lorraine.

"Mr. and Mrs. Pryor, could you come with me, please?" Detective DeCarlo asked while standing in the apartment's small kitchen. "We'd like you to try and identify the bodies."

Wanda Pryor could think of only one response: "Can Nancy come?" DeCarlo agreed, and Wanda began to ready herself for the trip to the morgue. As she collected her things, the possibility of having to see her youngest daughter's dead body before her own eyes finally set in. Wanda collapsed to the floor. Her family decided to take her to a doctor's office on Second Avenue before heading to the morgue.

"As soon as we left the apartment building, the media was all out there already," Nancy Pryor recalls. "I remember somebody shoving a microphone in my face and saying, 'How do you feel?' and I pushed him down, and said, *'How the fuck do you think I feel?'* Some of the reporters were grabbing my arm and saying, 'Come with us! Come with us! We'll give you a ride there!' because they wanted a story, but the detectives said, 'No, you're coming with *us*.' They drove us down the street so that my mother could visit the doctor there. The doctor gave my mother a shot of what I think was valium because she was just so distraught that she would not be able to answer any questions or anything."

The Pryor family then drove to the Bergen County Medical Examiner's Office in Paramus. "When we got there, there was this sea of reporters," Nancy Pryor says. "They all tried to stop me, but we just kept on walking. When my mother and I went in, my father waited in a separate area. He had a nervous disability, so we didn't let him go with us."

Wanda and Nancy Pryor were then presented with the jewelry that was found on the body suspected to be Mary Ann's. "Right away, I recognized the jewelry," Nancy says. "It was a chain with a little cross on it that her godfather had given her. There was also a little bracelet. I knew they were hers. That was eerie. I felt like this could really be them."

The two were then brought to the viewing room of an autopsy suite where a curtain covered a large window. "They opened the curtain. The body was covered with a sheet up to her face. I remember looking at her and saying, 'That's not my sister.' She had what looked like bruises on her face. She was in pretty bad shape. They said that the bodies had already

Mary Ann Pryor (left) and her sister Nancy in 1974. *Courtesy of Nancy Pryor.*

been dead for twenty-four to forty-eight hours. So I guess, at that point, the body was changing a little. It just didn't look like her. I mean, if you *really* looked at her, it did, but I wasn't *really* looking at her. I just really wanted to see the body there and know for sure whether or not it was her, and the person I was seeing just didn't look like her. I gasped and thought to myself, 'Maybe it's not her,' but it was. They didn't give me long to look, but after looking for a couple of more seconds, I realized that it was her. I knew from the jewelry, anyway. That was hard. The memory is still in my head, and I still have that cross."

In an adjacent viewing room, Thomas Kelly identified the second recovered body as that of his sister. Thomas, Maureen and Lorraine, along with another brother, John, were orphans. Their father, Thomas Sr., succumbed to emphysema in 1968, while their mother, Frances, had died of cancer only two months prior to her youngest daughter's murder. To further add to the tragedy of her killing, Lorraine Kelly's body was found only four days shy of her seventeenth birthday. According to friends and loved ones, the young woman was still deeply grieving her mother's death at the time of her disappearance.

Once she exited the Bergen County Medical Examiner's Office, Nancy Pryor immediately became a changed person. "I had to grow up real quick," she says. "I went from teenager to adult in two seconds, you know? I was the one handling the phone calls and all of the arrangements. My parents just couldn't talk to anyone. I had to take charge."

A shocked community stepped in to help the Pryor and Kelly families as Bergen County detectives continued their investigation. North Bergen's Vainieri Funeral Home stepped in and offered services to both families completely free of charge. Other organizations offered a reward for information leading to the arrest of the girls' killer. Acting on slightly inaccurate information, police in both Hudson and Bergen Counties began to mandatorily arrest hitchhikers. During an earlier interview with the *New York Daily News*, Wanda Pryor told reporters that Lorraine "likes to hitchhike." Other media publications ran with this quote, misprinting it as referring to Wanda's own daughter, Mary Ann. Soon after, even more newspapers began erroneously quoting Pryor as saying both girls liked to hitchhike. The *Bergen County Record* even went so far as to make the bold claim that, for Mary Ann and Lorraine, "hitchhiking was their pastime."

"I never knew of Mary Ann hitchhiking," says Sal Rubiano. "I never knew of a situation where she hitchhiked. Back in that era, hitchhiking was pretty common for us guys to get around sometimes. It was a different time where most of the time, it was pretty much safe for us. If we were going to a concert in Jersey City, a few of us guys might hitch a ride down there. We didn't think anything of it back then. We really weren't concerned about those things back then. But I don't know of any situation where Mary Ann hitched. Now, Lorraine was a little more outgoing, so maybe she had hitchhiked before, but I wouldn't be able to say for certain."

Two days after the discovery of the bodies, Dr. Lawrence Denson, Bergen County's chief medical examiner, made the determination that Mary Ann Pryor and Lorraine Kelly died as a result of suffocation. Dr. Denson theorized that Pryor and Kelly had been killed by their assailant placing something—possibly a hand, pillow or bag—over the mouths of the victims until they expired. Denson also concluded that the girls had been dead up to forty hours before they were discovered. This led investigators to believe that the bodies had been stored elsewhere for a period of time before being dumped, as Enis Perry noted that she had not seen anything lying in the wooded area near her apartment's parking lot the night before she made the discovery. Test results showed that Lorraine had most likely been killed six hours before Mary Ann. Burn marks, possibly from a cigarette, were also observed on the body of one of the teenagers. If the same person who had murdered Carol Farino, Jeannette DePalma and Joan Kramer had, in fact, killed Mary Ann and Lorraine, he had notably amplified the brutality of his modus operandi.

On Wednesday, August 21, 1974, after a week of forensic testing, the families of Mary Ann Pryor and Lorraine Kelly were finally able to hold a funeral for the slain girls. Over two hundred people lined the pews of the Our Lady of Fatima Roman Catholic Church in North Bergen. Reverend George O'Gorman stood in front of the two white caskets and offered a warning during the eulogy. "If Mary Ann and Lorraine could speak this morning," Reverend O'Gorman preached, "what a message they could give. Would not their words warn you of the loose and indiscriminate companionship of hitchhiking? Think and remember, so they will not have died in vain." After their funeral rites were performed, the bodies of Mary Ann Pryor and Lorraine Kelly were transported by hearse to their final resting places. Mary Ann was laid to rest in Hackensack's Saint Joseph's Cemetery, and Lorraine was reunited with her mother and father in Long Island National Cemetery.

Sal Rubiano never got to say goodbye to his first love, Mary Ann. "I did not stay for the funeral," he says, a somber tone filling his voice. "When I went up there, my head was in a damn cloud. Someone told me that the coroner was taking their time, and they didn't know when the funeral was going to be, so my parents said that maybe I should come home. I had this ring that I had given Mary Ann. It was from when I was in the service. It was an air force ring. Nancy told me that she would put the ring on a chain for Mary Ann to wear. She said she would make sure that Mary Ann was buried with that. I felt good about that, but it's a damn shock in your life that doesn't go away. You hold onto it your whole life. It never goes away. She was the first person in my life that loved me. When I was in the service, I would get letters from her every three or four days. When mail call came in, I had a letter from Mary Ann. She would take the time to find all of this different stationery. The papers would be in the shape of a heart and in all different colors. I would get eight- or nine-page letters from her, and the next time around, it would be a different kind of paper. On Valentine's Day that year, she had made me a heart-shaped cookie and sent it to me. I mean, by the time I got it, it was hard as a rock, but she sent that to me. That was the first relationship I was in where I felt like that person loved me, and I could do stupid things, and she would still be there."

As the weeks went on, the investigators from Hudson and Bergen County had less and less to go on. The reported sighting of the two girls in a Union City diner ended up being a false lead, as both girls' autopsy results conflicted with the waitress's story. Detectives checked out numerous locations that were suspected to be murder sites, but in the end, all turned out to be dead ends. Throughout their investigation, the Bergen County Prosecutor's Office was completely unaware of the similar murders of Carol Farino, Jeannette DePalma and Joan Kramer. Thanks to what many perceived as a police and media coverup, most people had forgotten all about these murders. However, in January 1975, the residents of South Orange would get a shocking reminder of the killing of Joan Kramer.

Mary Ann Pryor pictured only weeks before her death at the hands of a crazed killer. *Courtesy of Nancy Pryor.*

In the months since Otto Neil Nilson's August 1974 arrest for assaulting William Gregg and his two sons, the South Orange Police Department had conducted a vigilant investigation into the Maplewood accountant and his possible involvement in the murder of Joan Kramer. On January 9, 1975, Mary Colato, the fifty-three-year-old resident of South Orange who claimed to have witnessed a man pick up a female hitchhiker in South Orange Village on the night of Kramer's murder, was presented with a photograph of Nilson by detectives from the South Orange Police Department. After viewing the photograph, Colato identified the driver as Otto Neil Nilson. A judge issued an arrest warrant, and twenty-four hours later, on the night of Friday, January 10, investigators from the Essex County Prosecutor's Office knocked on the front door of Nilson's Maplewood apartment. As the forty-

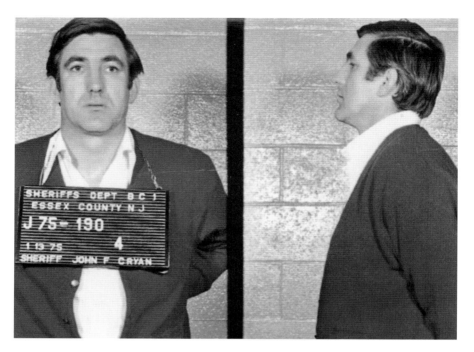

Otto Neil Nilson following his January 1975 arrest for the 1972 murder of Joan Kramer. *Courtesy of the South Orange Police Department.*

year-old opened the door, an officer withdrew his handcuffs and said, "Otto Neil Nilson, you are under arrest for the murder of Joan Kramer. You have the right to remain silent…"

The investigators drove Nilson to the Essex County Sheriff's Office for processing. He was arraigned three days later by county judge Julius Feinberg at the Essex County Courthouse annex in Newark. Nilson chose not to enter a plea. Judge Feinberg subsequently ordered the accused to be held without bail.

As Otto Neil Nilson sat in an Essex County jail cell, a disturbed fifteen-year-old boy armed with an axe crept into the dining room of his Mountainside home. Any semblance of normalcy that had survived in this community since the 1972 murder of Jeannette DePalma was about to be shattered.

10

THE AXE MURDERER

Secrets, silent, stony sit in the dark palaces of both our hearts: secrets weary of their tyranny: tyrants willing to be dethroned.
—*James Joyce,* Ulysses

The night of Saturday, January 14, 1975, was one marked by frigid temperatures, fog and occasional snow showers. These conditions, however, did not interfere with seventeen-year-old William Nelson's plans for that evening. Racing up Mountainside's Summit Road at upward of eighty miles per hour, Nelson and two other teenage friends were enjoying their weekend by living out the hot rod culture they so dearly admired. While the car sped toward the hilltop, a figure sliced through the glow of the vehicle's headlights. The driver quickly swerved out of the way and continued on its path.

"Hey, that's Gregg Sanders!" one youth shouted from the backseat. "Let's go knock some sense into him!" The driver declined to stop, and Nelson, along with his friends, continued on into the night. It was a decision they would be thankful to have made for years to come. Unbeknownst to the three youths at that time, Gregg Sanders was armed with a knife. The fifteen-year-old hypnotically made his way through the snow toward a 150-foot-tall water tower inside of the Watchung Reservation. Climbing the narrow staircase that snaked its way around the tower, the boy made his way to the top, slit his left wrist and jumped.

"Someone must have spotted the body and called the Union County Police," says retired Mountainside detective sergeant Jerome Rice. "I got

Fifteen-year-old Gregg Sanders leapt to his death from the top of this water tower inside of the infamous Watchung Reservation. *Photo by Mark Moran.*

a call about it around 11:00 p.m., and I showed up in plainclothes." Mountainside patrolman Jack Yerich had reported to the water tower moments earlier after four teenagers flagged him down, saying they had found a body lying about fifteen feet from the base of the tower. "There were two uniformed Union County officers there already at the scene," Rice continues. "I introduced myself and asked if they knew who the child was. They said no. They thought it was a murder. I said, 'No, this is a suicide.' I asked if they knew where the kid lived, and they said, 'No, we didn't touch the body.' I told them to back up. I went into his pocket and found a piece of paper with the name 'Sanders' on it. No first name. I don't know why he had it in his pocket. Seemed pretty reasonable if he wanted to be identified. Maybe that's why he had it. That's all he had, too. The name 'Sanders' didn't mean nothin' to me, so I called headquarters, and Lieutenant James Herrick said there was a Sanders family close by. This kid had to have walked there because there were no car or bicycle tracks. We got something out of one of the police cars, covered the body up and we continued the investigation."

Lieutenant Herrick theorized that the boy was most likely the son of Thomas and Janice Sanders of 1090 Sunny Slope Drive. Detective Sergeant Rice recalled this house as being only two blocks away from the home of the girl supposedly killed by devil worshippers in 1972. Rice can still recall the nefarious rumors surrounding the DePalma incident. "There was some voodoo-y bullshit found around the body there," he says. "Chicken bones and crap like that. I did not get involved in that. You know that guy, John List, who killed his whole family in Westfield? Well, he was one house removed from the Mountainside/Westfield border. Otherwise, he would have been my job. I showed up at the scene the night that they found the bodies. That was the closest that I got to the whole thing."

The forty-one-year-old detective sergeant decided to drive over to the Sanders residence along with Detective Sergeant Richard Mannix of the Union County Park Police. Less than three years prior, Mannix had been the first officer on the scene when John Hasenauer discovered the body of Joan Kramer. The two detectives decided to check in with a neighbor of the Sanders family before knocking on their door. "We wanted to check to see if the parents were in good health before we informed them of their son's suicide," Rice later wrote in his incident report. Once the detectives were told that neither parent suffered from a heart condition, the two made their way next door to the Sanders home. "I remember that well," Rice says. "I slipped on the ice checking the house out because their neighbors had turned their overhead lights out. I think Ritchie Mannix slipped, too." After ringing the doorbell and making several unanswered phone calls to Thomas and Janice Sanders, the two decided to attempt to gain entry via the rear of the house.

Entering the backyard of the Sanders residence, Rice and Mannix found the rear kitchen door open. Mannix stood in front of the doorway and yelled, "Mr. and Mrs. Sanders, this is Detective Sergeant Mannix of the Union County Park Police! Is anybody there?" When Mannix received no answer, he reached into the blackness beyond the open doorway and felt for a light switch. His fingers met two switches, and he turned on the outside lights along with the indoor kitchen lights. Suddenly, the body of Thomas Sanders was illuminated before him. He was lying on the ground in a pool of his own blood, a fifteen-inch axe buried in the side of his head. Not wanting to disturb the gruesome crime scene that lay before them, Rice and Mannix made their way back to the front of the house and forced open the front door. To the right of the entryway, the detectives found Janice Sanders lying on the dining room floor with blood pouring from several axe blows to her head. Rice went back to his car to notify the Union County Crime Lab and Dr. Bernard Ehrenberg, who was still serving as the county's medical examiner.

"It looked like Gregg had an argument with the father," Rice says. "Then he turned around while the father was sitting at the dining room table and came up behind him with the axe. He might have hit him once or twice. The father, even with being hit by the axe, got up, and either he started running away from the kid or he started chasing the kid because there was blood from the dining room to the front foyer, to the living room and then to the kitchen. He was hit there at least a total of five times. The mother heard the commotion. After the father collapsed in the kitchen, the kid went to the bottom of the stairs. When the mother came down, she went into the dining room where her husband was doing paperwork, and Gregg snuck up behind her. He hit her with the axe about twenty times. But he didn't have the strength that he had when he hit the father. These were lighter blows. More than enough to probably kill the poor woman after a few. The kid then buried the axe in the father's head."

As investigators searched the Sanders home, Detective Sergeant Rice found Gregg's bedroom. On a small desk, Rice found a handwritten note. It read:

To Whom It May Concern:
I am sorry for the trouble I have caused.
I am not in any way mad at my parents.
I just can't take it anymore.
Well, I just wanted to say I'm sorry.

Good Luck,
Gregg Sanders

Behind the desk, Rice noticed a small curtain covering the wall. "The kid must have popped a hole in the wall and put his desk in front of it," Rice says. "There was a curtain hanging down, so he must have just pushed the curtain aside, and he could go into the room. It wasn't a room, per se; it was the overhang of the house. They put up a wall, and the overhang was just there. There was bare rafters and stuff. It was kind of a crawlspace." Inside of this crawlspace, the detective made a shocking discovery. "All this bullshit was in there," Rice says. "All of his books on Adolf Hitler, pictures of the swastika, *Mein Kampf* and all that." Investigators also found a two-foot-high wooden panel made by Gregg that was inscribed with a large swastika and the words "*Amerikanische Nazi Partei.*" Also found were Nazi armbands, a six-page handwritten collection of Adolf Hitler quotes, a mattress, a lamp and several empty liquor bottles.

When we submitted an Open Public Records Act request to the Mountainside Police Department asking for the Sanders case file, we received a heavily redacted five-page report. Curiously missing from this report was any reference to the Nazi paraphernalia found in Gregg Sanders's bedroom. When we requested an itemized list of the evidence found inside the Sanders home, we were told by a municipal clerk that the "information requested is exempt from disclosure." When asked why such information was exempt, especially considering that the Mountainside Police Department had already released five pages of graphic crime scene reports without hesitation, the Borough of Mountainside had its law firm, Post, Polak, Goodsell, MacNeill and Strauchler, P.A., send us a notice claiming that "no such a report" of crime scene evidence appears in the "Borough file." Attorney John N. Post then expressed his "hope" that we would not file an appeal based on his firm's decision. Despite this, we believe Jerome Rice's account of the discovery of these items to be true.

In addition to the gruesome details of Gregg's parents' murder, descriptions of his secret Nazi shrine were leaked to the press as well. As if a suicide following a double axe murder were not enough to completely horrify the communities of Mountainside and Springfield, the news of a teenage Nazi sympathizer walking in their midst for years seemed to prove that things would never be the same in the quiet suburbia of Union County.

"I believe the uneasiness caused by the DePalma incident had calmed down quite a bit by the time the Sanders incident happened," says former Mountainside resident Roy Simpson. Simpson knew Gregg personally, and they even played on the same baseball team together. "He was on my Little League team about two years before he killed his parents and himself. I wasn't particularly close friends with him, but I remember him. What I remember about him—and this is one of the reasons why I was not particularly close friends with him—is him being kind of a wise guy. He was kind of a bully. I remember him being kind of, you know, a wise kid. A wisecracker, I guess. Maybe even a little bit on the *cruel* side. There were rumors going around town that there were two Nazi-sympathizing families in Mountainside and that the Sanders family was one of them. My sister, who was in high school at the time, had mentioned this rumor to me right around the time of the Sanders incident. It might have been before; it might have been after. It certainly was the talk among the townsfolk. I don't feel comfortable saying the name of the other family because I never heard any verification. It's a horrible thing to say about a family. When this happened with Gregg, I believe that the police found a bunch of Nazi paraphernalia that he had in a little tiny cubbyhole, or something like that, in his room."

"At that time, Mountainside was, and probably still is, very *Leave It to Beaver*," Mary Starr recalls. "It was a very quiet, intellectual, middle-class community. It was a very nice place to grow up. You did not have *extremes*. To have something like *this* happen, particularly because there were a number of Holocaust survivors who lived in Mountainside, it just shook the town. We were just flabbergasted. We had nothing like Skokie. We had nothing like skinheads or neo-Nazis. That was something we only saw on the news. Not here. Not in our town. To have something like that come out was absolutely shocking. We were all stunned. We all thought Gregg was a little weird and was not the nicest person in the world, but we didn't think he was capable of this. I'm not a psychologist of any kind, and I don't pretend to be one, but this had all the hallmarks of someone snapping and going over the edge. Nowadays, he might have been a kid who would have just grabbed an AR-15 and started shooting. It amazed us that he could have set up this shrine without his parents knowing. Then again, kids that age can be very secretive."

The residents of Mountainside and Springfield began to look for answers to why and how something as horrific as this could have happened. "Gregg was around three or four years younger than me," William Nelson recalls. "He didn't attend any of the local schools. His parents wanted him to be at Pingry, which was a private school in Hillside. He had a sister named Wendy who was around my older sister's age. My sister knew her, but not real well. From what I understand, Mr. Sanders started working as a maintenance man in a bank when he was a young man. He started at the low end of the totem pole. He eventually worked himself all the way up to becoming the president of the bank. He had high aspirations for his children. My understanding was that Mr. Sanders and his wife were very strict. Gregg and Wendy were not given a lot of freedom. They were required by their parents to study very hard. Mr. Sanders went from nothing to being the president of this bank, and I guess he wanted his children to have the same opportunities that he had. So the kids constantly had to study. If Wendy wanted to go to a party down the street, she wasn't allowed to. That is the situation that the Sanders family was going through, as far as I understand. I never saw Gregg outside of his house a whole lot. Not a lot of people had the opportunity to really know him because he wasn't the 'normal' kid of the neighborhood. In those days, if you were a kid, you were out all day long, playing with your friends and having a good time going from one house to another. That wasn't something that Gregg and Wendy were allowed to do. They were required to be in the house studying and learning, so we really didn't have a lot of interaction with that family. The only time you got to see Gregg and Wendy was in the morning at the bus stop. My younger brother went to Pingry for a while. He knew Gregg a little better. As far as my brother was concerned, Gregg was a little strange. *Eccentric*, I would say, but I don't think anybody saw anything like this coming at all. To find out, after the fact, that Gregg had a crawlspace in the attic of the house where he kept his little shrine and Nazi propaganda—*that* was a shock. He was never known to have any strange likings for things like that. That was something that nobody seemed to know about or was really talked about. As far as we knew, he was just a poor kid that was kept inside his house all the time."

Denise Parker also remembers Gregg Sanders. "He was a little, skinny kid," she recalls. "My ex-boyfriend went to Pingry with him. He was the one being whipped by the bullies before Gregg got there because he was a professional ice dancer and was very, very metrosexual. He told me that his life became manageable once Gregg showed up at Pingry because the bullies shifted their focus from him onto Gregg. He felt bad for him, but his life changed so much. Everybody stopped picking on him and went to Gregg." Parker also recalls her own personal connection to Gregg's last night on earth. "He walked right in front of my house and up my driveway on his way to commit suicide," she says.

Teen uses ax to slay parents, leaps to death

By RICHARD CONNIFF

A quiet Mountainside youth methodically and without apparent motive murdered his mother and father with an ax, then leaped to his death from a nearby water tower late Tuesday night, police said.

Gregg Sanders, 15, a bright but shy sophomore at the Pingry School in Hillside, reportedly sat down about 9 p.m. in his bedroom at 1090 Sunny Slope Dr. and wrote — in a note addressed "To whom it may concern" — that he was sorry for what he was about to do.

He then went downstairs, found an ax and attacked his father, first at the dining room table where he was working and then as the parent staggered through the lower floor of the house, police said.

After Thomas Sanders Jr.,

48, had fallen dead on the kitchen floor, police said, the youth attacked his mother, Janice L. Sanders, 44, when she came downstairs. He left her dead on the dining room floor, with a single ax blow.

Police said Sanders then shut out the first-floor lights of the house and left by the kitchen door. Despite the freezing temperature, he walked without a jacket or coat the 10-minute route up to the 150-foot water tower in the Watchung Reservation.

The teenager climbed the winding staircase to the top of the tower, then slit one wrist deeply and leaped, headfirst, to the ground, authorities reported.

The double murder-suicide left only one member of the Sanders family, Wendy, 18. She had left the family home

Thomas Sanders Jr.
Respected bank exec

Gregg Sanders
'A nice boy'

to live and work in Revere, Mass., outside Boston.

Neighbors and friends of Sanders, who had been a vice president of First National City Bank in New York, his wife, who had directed and taught at a church nursery school, and the youth searched their minds yesterday for some clue that might have warned them about what was to happen.

"He was a nice boy," said Mrs. Betty Roche, a neighbor.

"Otherwise, I wouldn't have let my son play with him. He was as happy and normal a boy as you can imagine, from kindergarten up to now. I didn't see any tension in his life. It must have been something behind closed doors."

Dennis Sargenti, a 17-year-old friend and neighbor of the youth, called the Sanderses "a decent family" and said the youth was "super-smart in school."

● ● ●

The shocking news of Gregg Sanders's final acts made headlines across the United States. *Collection of the authors.*

"I was on the scene the day that his body was found. I actually followed his footprints in the snow all the way to the tower. I went up there, and his brains were within a fifty-yard radius. There was a dent in the ground where his head hit, and his brains were scattered like an umbrella all through the woods. There was blood everywhere. They said that he cut his wrists before he jumped, so I was trying to find the knife or whatever he cut his wrists with. I figured he threw it, so I was trying to be the hero and find the weapon, but I never did."

"Gregg was a brilliant, brilliant kid," Mary Starr says. "He was nerdy, and unfortunately, the nerds were the ones who got picked on. He was shy, but he was also a bully. He did a lot of acting out, and I bet that was because of what was going on with his family, especially with his dad. You know, kids who are victims of whatever kind of abuse will act out and will sometimes act out in very inappropriate ways. I am assuming Gregg acted out by bullying others simply to deal with the pain inside of himself because he had no control over what was going on at home. He wanted control over others. He wasn't the nicest person in the world. I remember telling him to leave the younger kids alone at one point. Once he started at Pingry, however, I did not see him all that much. I remember him more from before he went to Pingry. Pingry was, and probably still is, very competitive and very elitist, but at the same time, Gregg was also elitist. He liked to throw around the fact that he was smarter than everybody else. I also knew his sister Wendy, who was two or three years ahead of me. She and I took piano lessons from the same teacher. We spent an hour together every week, but it was a didactic situation, and we did not talk all that much. She was a nice girl and pretty talented. I think she survived only because she was in college when this all happened. I remember hearing that she changed her name fairly quickly because I'm sure she was being hounded and just wanted to disappear. Can you imagine having to deal with that for the rest of your life? It was so incredibly sensational."

At Gregg's autopsy, Dr. Bernard Ehrenberg was able to conclude that the teenager had not been under the influence of alcohol or drugs of any kind when he murdered his parents. Eventually, the bodies of Thomas, Janice and Gregg Sanders were cremated, and a small memorial service was held in the garden of the Mountainside Community Memorial Church. Once the Mountainside Police Department's investigation was concluded, the Sanders home at 1090 Sunny Slope Drive was thoroughly cleaned and put up for sale. Lastly, the stairs leading to the top of the water tower along the Sierra Trail inside of the Watchung Reservation were permanently removed. For decades, the tower had been a popular lover's lane where teenagers could enjoy themselves in private, all while gazing in awe at the Manhattan skyline. With his suicide, Gregg Sanders ensured that no one would ever be afforded this particular pleasure again.

In the wake of the List murders, the killing of Jeannette DePalma and now the Sanders incident, the residents of Union County began to wonder if a curse had somehow been laid on the land. Many feared that the communities of Westfield, Springfield and Mountainside could never return to the Norman Rockwell image of middle-class suburban paradise that they once were.

"The Sanders murder definitely cast a large shadow over Mountainside," Roy Simpson says. "It was definitely a hard thing to squelch. I mean, how many years ago was Lizzie Borden? People still talk about that. But I do remember that the talk about the DePalma case died out really quickly, especially for something as shocking as the murder of a young girl. I have to admit that was odd."

Hank Warner agrees with Simpson's sentiment. "The police in this town never did anything about that case," he says. "It's a shame because somebody on the police force or detective force has an idea of who did kill her. Somebody didn't do their homework or follow through on this, or they

The metal staircase that wrapped around this water tower was removed shortly after Gregg Sanders leapt to his death from the top step. *Photo by Jesse P. Pollack.*

just shut the book and forgot about her. They swept something under the rug about this. I'm just telling you, it just seems kind of peculiar that this was never, ever settled. If the detectives did their homework, they would find out who did this."

"People freely talked about it in town for about two weeks, and then it was never mentioned again," Roy Simpson continues. "It was never, *never* brought up in school. The neighborhood gossip died a very, very quick death. That probably didn't strike me as very odd at the time because I was busy being an eleven-year-old and doing things like playing ball in the street, but now I do find it very odd that it was swept under the rug so quickly. You know, as a father, I can't even imagine. If my daughter died under mysterious circumstances, I would be all over the news trying to find out what's going on. I now live in a town that's very similar to Mountainside, and if something like that happened in our town right now, it would be the talk of the town for *years*. So, as an adult looking back, it's strange. *Very* strange."

11

THE TRIAL

Nothing is more wretched than the mind of a man conscious of guilt.
—*Titus Maccius Plautus*

On Wednesday, July 9, 1975, the homicide trial against Otto Neil Nilson finally commenced. Anthony R. Mautone, Essex County's assistant prosecutor, began his opening statements by highlighting the fact that while no one had witnessed Joan Kramer's murder, she had been seen entering Nilson's car on the night of her death. "It would be reasonable to infer that the man who picked her up at 12:30 [a.m.] is the man who killed her," he said. "Just as if you walked into the kitchen and found a jam jar open and your little boy with jam all over his face, you don't need any direct evidence to know that he was in the jam. That's the way this case is."

John Cleary, Nilson's public defender, tried to garner sympathy for the defendant during his opening statements. "Let's not make it two victims," Cleary urged the jurors. "Let's not make Otto Nilson the second victim. You're going to have to listen and not form any conclusions until you've heard all the evidence. You have to appreciate the quality of the testimony, not the quantity. Is it credible or incredible?"

Problems arose almost immediately. During the six months that he spent in prison, Nilson grew a thick, scruffy beard. This presented significant trouble, as Mary Colato, the prosecution's star witness, had allegedly observed Nilson as clean-shaven on the night of Joan Kramer's murder. At a pretrial hearing two days before, Essex County Superior Court judge

Sam A. Colarusso had requested that the defendant shave before arriving in court the next day. Nilson declined.

Despite his refusal to shave his beard, Colato still identified Nilson as the man who had picked up a hitchhiking woman at 12:05 a.m. on the night Kramer vanished. Incensed by this seemingly unlikely positive identification, John Hughes, an assistant deputy public defender acting as part of Nilson's legal counsel, asked South Orange detective Anthony Fabrizio on the stand if Colato had taken a polygraph test. Fabrizio recalled Colato taking one such test but could not remember the exact date. The prosecution then pointed out that not only had Otto Neil Nilson taken a polygraph examination himself, but he had also failed this particular test when questioned about Joan Kramer's murder.

Cleary blasted Colato's testimony as "dangerous and frightening." The public defender openly asked the court how the witness could "get an identification on him in the space of one traffic light." Colato insisted that she could identify Nilson in that amount of time—and after nearly three years—due to the fact that the defendant had approached her inside of Adam's Tavern on Forest Street in the city of Orange earlier on the evening in question. Colato, who was having drinks in the tavern, claimed that Nilson had approached her at the bar and offered to buy her a round. She allegedly declined this gesture. When asked by the defense if she recognized Nilson as being an usher at Our Lady of Sorrows Church in South Orange, which also happened to be Colato's parish of choice, she replied in the negative but was quick to point out that she did not attend services very often. Colato also told the court that she had observed a South Orange police officer enter the Bun 'N' Burger restaurant on Sloan Street while she was sitting next to Nilson at the traffic light and that this officer could corroborate her story.

South Orange patrolman Stanley B. Dalton was called to the witness stand on Monday, July 14, 1975. During his testimony, Dalton denied ever being anywhere near the Bun 'N' Burger on the night of Kramer's murder. The patrolman told the court that he had actually checked himself into Orange Memorial Hospital for an eight-day stay on August 14, 1972, a full day before the incident in question. In a significant blow to Colato's testimony, Officer Dalton produced medical records that supported his claim. Today, however, the Kramer family remains unconvinced. "Dalton perjured himself," says Orin Kramer. "He snuck out of treatment at the hospital and saw the whole thing. He tried to cover it up."

Nilson's neighbor, Curt Knoth, has similar recollections: "Stan Dalton was a drunk and a dirty cop."

To this day, many who were close to or involved with the Kramer case feel that Dalton was faced with a difficult choice. Rumors about Dalton's alleged alcoholism were flaunted around South Orange, and some feel that this led to his admission into Orange Memorial Hospital for treatment. Some allege that he was able to sneak out of the hospital undetected for a drink at the Bun 'N' Burger only one day after becoming a patient, and this was when he had witnessed Kramer entering Nilson's car. Those who subscribe to this theory believe that Dalton feared losing his job and pension if he admitted to breaking out of Orange Memorial Hospital to drink, so he chose to deny the allegations while on the witness stand.

Despite Dalton's testimony, Colato continued to maintain that Otto Neil Nilson was the man who had pulled up alongside her at the intersection of Sloan Street and South Orange Avenue on the night of August 15, 1972, and that he had given a ride to a young woman who said she lived on top of the hill. Colato claimed the she could not identify the woman as being Joan Kramer, as the woman was standing outside of her field of vision.

One witness who could identify the young woman as Kramer, however, was James Tillett, a former security guard. Tillett had been working at a South Orange apartment complex on the night of August 15, 1972. After his shift ended, Tillett walked down the north side of South Orange Avenue in order to catch a bus ride home to Newark. While walking toward the bus stop near the train trestle at the Sloan Street intersection, Tillett claimed that he observed a young woman wearing an evening gown walking on the same side of South Orange Avenue. When shown a photograph of Joan Kramer, Tillett remarked that there was "no doubt" in his mind that she was the same young woman. The former security guard was also able to correctly identify the clothing that Kramer had worn on the night of her murder. Tillett then testified that he watched as Kramer walked quickly across the street and approached a car that was stopped at the traffic light beneath the train trestle. According to Tillett, some words were exchanged, and then Kramer entered the vehicle. Tillett told the court that he got a good look at the vehicle and its operator. "He was dressed up real nice," Tillett said. "A real together dude." He went on to describe the driver as being clean-shaven with dark hair and a jacket. Tillett estimated that the man was somewhere around thirty to thirty-five years old and that he resembled a businessman. Tillett, however, could not positively identify the driver of the car as being Otto Neil Nilson. While he "favored" Nilson as the man he saw picking up Joan Kramer three years earlier, he pointed out that the driver of that vehicle was clean-shaven while the defendant before him was bearded.

In addition to Mary Colato, one other person in the courtroom happened to recognize Otto Neil Nilson: Julian Kramer. "When Nilson was brought into the courtroom, my father looked at me and said, 'I know that man,'" Orin Kramer recalls. "I asked my father how he knew this person, and he told me that after my sister had been killed, this man had directly delivered some papers to him at his office in Newark."

As Julian Kramer and his son watched from their seats inside the courtroom, James Tillett continued with his testimony. Tillett told the court that he had seen Joan Kramer enter a dark green car with a vinyl top and that this vehicle was in "very good shape." Mary Colato described Nilson's car as being either "dark green or dark blue" but could not discern whether the automobile was a hardtop or a convertible.

In fact, Nilson did own a green 1964 four-door Buick at the time of Joan Kramer's murder. However, investigators were not able to examine this vehicle due to the fact that Nilson had traded it into an automotive dealer three months after Joan Kramer and Jeannette DePalma disappeared. Joan's family viewed this act as very suspicious.

In response to Tillett's and Colato's testimonies, the defense called three witnesses to the stand, each claiming that Otto Neil Nilson's Buick did not have a vinyl top, nor was it in "very good shape." Eugene Insogna, a former co-worker of Nilson's, recalled the Buick as being "beat-up." John Waddell, a representative of the Buick Motor Division, testified that the model belonging to the defendant did not feature a vinyl top. Alexander Alves, whose Jersey City auto dealership agreed to take the Buick toward a trade, recalled that he had valued the vehicle at a mere twenty-five dollars due to its condition.

As the specifics of Otto Neil Nilson's green Buick were being discussed during the trial, no one in attendance could have known that a green Buick had featured heavily in a haunting vision experienced by the cousin of Jeannette DePalma, the girl from Springfield who had been killed one week before Joan and only six miles away. In addition, it may never be known whether the prosecution was even aware of the murders of Jeannette DePalma, Mary Ann Pryor and Lorraine Kelly or their many similarities to the killing of Joan Kramer. Anthony Mautone did not respond to requests for comment, and when we sought the transcripts of the Kramer homicide trial from the Essex County Prosecutor's Office, we were told that after an "intensive" fourteen-day search of the office's off-site storage facility, no records of the trial, Otto Neil Nilson or Joan Kramer's homicide could be located, and all were presumed lost or destroyed. We were told the same thing by the Union County Police, formerly the Union County Park Police, when we requested Detective Sergeant Richard Mannix's incident report documenting John Hasenauer's discovery of Joan Kramer's body.

On Tuesday, July 15, 1975, the prosecution and defense in the trial against Otto Neil Nilson gave their final summations. John Cleary, Nilson's public defender, told the jury that Mary Colato was "dangerously mistaken" when she identified his client as the man who had picked up Joan Kramer on the night of her murder and implored them to cease to the "six-month nightmare" that the former accountant had endured in jail since January. Cleary also went on to demean Joan's family by implying that Nilson had been arrested only because Essex County investigators wanted to bring an end to the pain felt by the wealthy and popular Kramers. "I think because of the nature of this case and the prominence of the girl, the prosecutor's office felt under pressure to make at least some arrests and charge someone with the offense, especially after the length of time involved," Cleary said.

Assistant Essex County prosecutor Anthony Mautone deflected Cleary's criticisms by reminding the jurors that James Tillett had positively identified Kramer and her clothing and that any complications regarding Mary Colato's identification of Otto Neil Nilson could be boiled down to the fact that the defendant refused to shave his beard after being instructed to do so by Judge Colarusso. Mautone also cited Joan's autopsy report, which stated that she had been killed less than two hours after eating dinner at her family's home in South Orange. "The person who picked up Joan Kramer is the person who murdered her," he said. "There was no time for anyone else."

After Cleary and Mautone concluded their closing statements, the jury began its deliberations. Judge Colarusso barred the twelve jurors from returning a first-degree murder conviction, as he was not convinced that Kramer's murder was premeditated. Two hours of heated discussion among the jurors passed without a verdict being reached, so Colarusso decided to dismiss the seven men and five women until the following morning. He instructed them to act as if they were sequestered, not speaking with the media or reading any newspaper accounts of the trial proceedings. Several reporters observed two of the female jurors leaving the courthouse in tears. No explanation for this incident was ever given.

On Wednesday, July 16, 1975, the twelve jurors in the trial against Otto Neil Nilson reconvened. About 2:30 p.m., after hours of further deliberation, the jury delivered its verdict: *not guilty*. Tillett's failure to positively identify Nilson, along with Colato's failure to identify the victim, had effectively destroyed any chance of the jury finding that the defendant had, beyond any shadow of a doubt, killed Joan Kramer. The testimony of Patrolman Stanley Dalton did not help the situation, either. After the verdict was read, Nilson quietly leaned toward Cleary and whispered, "Thank you. Thank you very much."

Otto Neil Nilson was immediately released from custody and found his mother, Helen, waiting on the steps of the Essex County Courthouse. Also waiting was a crowd of reporters, all eager for a comment. "I'm glad it's over," he told them. "It's hard to adjust to freedom after you've been locked up so long. Right now, all I'm concerned about is that I'm outside and I feel fairly well. I'm just glad that it's over. As soon as I saw the jury come in, I felt pretty good." When asked what he was doing on the night of the murder, Nilson told reporters, "I can't say for sure what I was doing that night, but I know I was at least twenty miles away in Jersey City, where I was living at the time."

"He was full of shit!" Curt Knoth says. "Nilson was living in Union with his mother at the time." Dr. Sari Kramer also recalls being told that her sister's alleged murderer had been residing in Union in August 1972.

If the recollections of Curt Knoth and Dr. Sari Kramer are accurate, that would mean that Otto Neil Nilson was much closer to Jeannette DePalma at the time of her murder, as the township of Union borders Springfield. This piece of information also sheds significant light on a statement made to us by Jeannette's best friend, Gail Donohue.

"Where Jeannette's body was found is on the opposite side of the way you would take to get to my house in Berkeley Heights," she says. However, if the driver who picked up Jeannette was planning to take the hitchhiker to Union, this person very well could have taken the route past the Houdaille Quarry on Mountview Road on the way to State Highway 82. By this point, Jeannette would have been more than aware that she was being taken somewhere other than her intended destination and could have bailed out of the driver's car in order to flee into the woods—much like Joan Kramer would do one week later near Union's Salem Road.

Gail Donohue definitely believes this to be possible. "That would account for the distribution of her pocketbook items," she says through tears. "The fact that her possessions were found strewn near her body gave me nightmares because I knew she was running. She was running for her life, and she *knew*. It wasn't just an immediate...like, she didn't

A common road sign takes on an ominous meaning here on Mountview Road. *Photo by Jesse P. Pollack.*

know what happened or what came over her; her last minutes had to be straight and total *terror*, and that kills me. Jeannette always had lipstick and a compact, and they were found in a row leading to her body because she was running. That's what always gnawed at me; she knew what was coming. That feeling ate at me for years. She was running for her life. I'm firmly convinced of it. Jeannette was a tough cookie. I mean, I was a priss compared to Jeannette. She would put her hands on her hips and say, '*Don't mess with me or I'll mess you up.*' I was the complete opposite. So for her to be scared, she had to have been scared out of her bloody wits and 150 percent certain, otherwise she would have done something to that person…"

Despite Nilson's verdict of not guilty, Essex County prosecutor Joseph P. Lordi felt that the right man had been put on trial and considered the Kramer case unofficially closed. "Whether or not I reopen the case depends on any additional evidence that comes to my attention," Lordi told reporters. Despite Lordi's opinion that Nilson was, in fact, guilty of murdering Joan Kramer, the freed former accountant would never again face prosecution for the young woman's murder. Double jeopardy laws would see to that.

"When Nilson got off, I remember my father or my uncle telling us that the witness, Mary Colato, moved to California because she was so scared that he was back on the streets," Billy Gregg recalls.

After being acquitted of a high-profile murder, Otto Neil Nilson seemingly had a new lease on life as a free man. However, the Joan Kramer trial would not be the last time the forty-year-old former accountant would find himself in a courtroom.

12

AFTERMATH

Where there is mystery, it is generally suspected there must also be evil.
—Lord Byron

E arly on the morning of Monday, September 13, 1976, Otto Neil Nilson walked through the doors of the East Orange Veterans Administration Hospital. In his hands, he held a high-powered rifle. The forty-one-year-old Nilson paced through the hospital's lobby until he came upon Dr. Florence Rock and Dr. Jean Louis. Raising his weapon, Nilson ordered the two physicians into a security office. Barricading himself and his two hostages inside the room, the manic rifleman began to rant and rave about a "conspiracy" that was preventing him from seeing his five children, all of whom were still living with their mother. Eventually, the Federal Bureau of Investigation was called in to handle the hostage situation, and after four tense hours of negotiation, Nilson surrendered and was immediately apprehended. He had been a free man for less than fourteen months.

Faced with an eight-count federal indictment, Nilson went to trial in July of the following year. Dr. Steven Simring, along with Dr. Seymour Kuvin, testified that the defendant was suffering from paranoid schizophrenia. In fact, this diagnosis had already been discussed with Nilson during his stay at Overbrook Asylum three years prior. In two letters addressed to the judge who had ordered him to undergo the psychiatric evaluation, Nilson discussed this proposed diagnosis. We were able to obtain copies of these letters through the South Orange Police Department.

The first letter, handwritten on ruled paper, was dated August 12, 1974—three days after Mary Ann Pryor and Lorraine Kelly disappeared—and read:

OTTO NEIL NILSON, C.P.A.
173 Maplewood Avenue
Maplewood, N.J. 07040

Dear Judge Pfifer,
I write this letter only because I feel you probably are the only person at this time who can do justice to this situation.

My name is Otto Neil Nilson, a person who appeared before you some weeks ago. At that time you ordered me to see a psychiatrist and to stay out of South Orange. Awaiting a judgment from the psychiatrist as to my mental stability I have decided to do some self-education and if I may, please refer to my following self-analysis:

Cause of breaking, entering & assault: The day before I broke into the house I had been experimenting in my capacity to drink; I consumed over 2/3 of a fifth of Seagram's gin, over a half a fifth of dry vermouth, over half a fifth sweet vermouth, and about a ½ pint of scotch within five minutes—this was done to see what my capacity was to be able to work while intoxicated, immediately I remember I started to write, then vomited and went to sleep. The effect really did not come until the next day and you know the result—the main thought is that the action was delayed about 24 hours. When I was first brought into the hospital I had forgotten this incident because of the effects of the liquor.

In addition to this I have been hospitalized under the label "schizophrenia," which I realize is a term for delayed effects of alcohol consumption.

Reason for the above statement—Since I was about 17, I was hyper active, during the summer, the time was spent swimming & working (throwing 100 lb. ice blocks to a grinder 5' above ground)—during the period of school I attended school on a full time basis and still worked two jobs and ended with a "B" average. All during this period I worked and drank beer on seldom occasions, once in a while I would become intoxicated and laugh and sing—During my marriage I concentrated on mental work with little physical exercise, but drank occasionally, usually with food, however during 1969 I had started my own practice had very little activity physically—as a result,— this now is assumptive—I think that the (1) alcohol was stored and broke down the protein needed for my brain to function (2) or else the alcohol stored as much energy in the cells that hallucinations occurred, after which followed a series of depressions—I first caught a bad cold which lasted during the winter—however I still drank—but never to excess—I always enjoyed dancing and drinking which was a release to the brain But still I think alcohol must still lie dormant for awhile [sic]—this alcohol still was still active without my knowing. As of today I feel fine and don't expect this to occur again.

(3) Psychiatrist—I am presently attending Mt. Carmel Guild in a group session—the session brings about nine people together to discuss problems, mostly it appears to me now—these problems relate to alcohol—I never studied about except for the past few days when I read a few chapters in Micro Biology. It appears that the following occurs in alcohol:

(Here, Nilson hand drew a diagram of a protein cell being destroyed by alcohol.)

My impression here is that more jelly cells replace the destroyed jelly cells and affect the alcohol (which may extinguish itself because of rotting itself away) and as a result the jelly cells cause hallucinations because they multiply too fast.

Now the point of the above is to come to a second point—they expect me to take Thorazine (I researched this and am submitting this from the Encyclopedia Britannica—I would have exhausted this more at Seton Hall Library but I'm not permitted in South Orange. I use the Thorazine *as a sleeping pill now—but in the hospital the Thorazine felt like acid when I drank it in orange juice—I had to have at least four glasses of water to wash down the pain.*

Thank you for reading this letter, while I was in Overbrook, I talked with a few people whose troubles were really never listened to, and these people are really in a dilemma. One person was being given medication because he had amnesia (about 33 years of age). If it was Thorazine—I never asked—this may be contributing to his problem.

I am enclosing the prints from the encyclopedia—I marked the important ones here in red.

Respectfully
Otto Nilson

The second letter, dated November 16, 1974, went on to say:

Dear Judge Pfifer:

This is in addition to my first letter—the reason again is that there seems no one to present these findings to whom has any authority. In my first letter I mentioned Thorazine—Yesterday I went to my weekly meeting and found that most of the people suffered from the same problem as I—alcohol. One woman was institutionalized for over six years and is in an awful way, she twitched when the psychiatrist asked her questions and her answers were stuttered—I talked to her awhile and talked approvingly and she stopped stuttering after awhile [sic] *and talked evenly, however, she reverted back to the twitch when the psychiatrist spoke to her; she had been on Thorazine for years. A man (large) was kept under Thorazine for 1½ years. He appeared alright (now stuttering or twitching).*

This morning, one of my students at college asked me for extra help—it seems he has trouble with examinations—I gave him an I.Q. test and when questions of memory or judgment came about he would yawn and become relaxed, when perceptive questions were asked he answered quickly and correctly. This led me to ask if he was taking drugs (illegible side insert here) and he told me he was taking Stelazine. This drug only affects certain parts of the mental process—but it appears to me if people in these conditions were put into a gymnasium or given some manual labor and only given water and basic foods, a lot of these problems would be eliminated, instead the psychiatrists prescribe drugs which cause the person to become almost vegetable. One man said he had been drinking and started to walk around the block about ten times but was picked up and put into the hospital and given drugs. Possibly if there was a gymnasium where these people would have to work out each day to drain the alcohol and give them only water, the basic problem would be brought to light because the person would be alert and his memory would not be impaired and no damage would be done to him.

These are a few ideas I have had, next week the caffeine problem people will be the subject of the discussion.

Respectfully
Otto Nilson

In each of these bizarre letters, Nilson blamed his experimentations with the consumption of alcohol for his violent behavior, all while shunning the medication prescribed by the doctors at Overlook. The former accountant's second letter mentions "one of my students at college" asking for "extra help," leading the reader to believe that Nilson somehow acquired a teaching job at an unnamed college. However, we could not verify this implied claim.

On Thursday, July 21, 1977, Essex County judge Felix Martino ruled that Otto Neil Nilson was suffering from a "disease of the mind" and therefore had the potential to do serious harm to himself and others. Psychiatrists testifying on behalf of both the prosecution and the defense all agreed that the forty-two-year-old former accountant was legally insane. Judge Martino sentenced Nilson to be committed to Trenton Psychiatric Hospital until future order of the court. For many, Otto Neil Nilson's reign of terror seemed to finally be over.

"I remember the Kramer murder later being the cover story for one of those cheesy police magazines like *True Detective*, *True Crime* or something like that," Daniel Gregg recalls. "The cover had the typical graphic of a terrified sexy female on the ground, complete with torn dress, looking up toward a huge man's shadow that was looming over her. The headline was something like 'Joan's Hair Was Blonde Bait for the Strangler.' Someone gave my dad a copy years ago, but I have no idea if it's still lying around somewhere. The Kramer murder was also an early story in Geraldo Rivera's career. I remember him in the alley in the village, reporting, '[A]nd this was the payphone Joan used before getting into the car...'"

In the early 1980s, only a few years after Otto Neil Nilson's committal, Jeannette DePalma's older sister, Carole, began to seek counseling for emotional issues. She found a psychiatrist by the name of Mary in Phillipsburg and began seeing her for regular sessions. Around three weeks into seeing this doctor, Carole began to mention that her younger sister, Jeannette, had been murdered several years earlier. Her psychiatrist immediately ended the session, telling Carole that she was "treating someone involved" with her sister's case and that she would have to seek treatment elsewhere. Carole was never given any further explanation regarding who this "involved" patient might have been.

Spurred on by this incident, and by years of being stonewalled by the Springfield Police Department, Florence DePalma hired a private investigator to look into her daughter's death. "He came up with nothing, a complete dead end," an anonymous member of the DePalma family wrote in a 2004 letter to *Weird NJ* magazine. "His conclusion was a cover up." Florence hired a second private investigator, but this man died of a heart attack before his work could be concluded. Feeling defeated, the DePalma family began to slowly accept the idea that they might never find answers regarding who had killed Jeannette.

While Florence was dealing with the frustration brought on by the lack of new leads, her daughter Gwendolyn was living on her own in Hillsborough with her three children. Neither Gwendolyn nor her young children could have been prepared for the shocking visit that a man with a gun was about to pay them.

"This was around 1984," says Gwendolyn's daughter, Racheal Sajeski. "We lived on a second-floor apartment at that time. It had steps inside of the apartment that went downstairs to a door, and that door led to a hallway. I was around nine years old at the time. I went downstairs to grab the mail, and there was this man standing in our doorway." According to Racheal, the man wore a solid green military field coat and jeans. He had dark, thinning hair and wore glasses. Racheal shuddered as she noticed the man before her clutching a rifle equipped with a silencer. "He started asking me all these questions like, 'Who lives here?' 'What's your name?' 'Are you sure *that's* who lives here?' and stuff like that. He just kept repeating himself. I stood there for what seemed like fifteen minutes, but it was probably less than that."

After a few minutes had gone by, Gwendolyn DePalma noticed that her daughter still had not returned from their downstairs mailbox. Sticking her head into the hallway, she heard Racheal conversing with the mysterious man.

"Who are you talking to?" she yelled.

"Mom, it's a man with a gun…" Racheal replied.

Terrified, Gwendolyn shouted for her daughter to run back up the steps. Racheal slammed the door shut but almost immediately felt the gunman try to force his way through. Struggling, she attempted to lock the deadbolt on the door. After a few seconds, she gave up and raced back up to her apartment. Panicking, Gwendolyn collected her other two children, and the shaken family made their way toward the apartment's balcony. Once outside, Gwendolyn and her children watched as the gunman fled down the street. Satisfied that he was not going to immediately return, Gwendolyn called the Hillsborough Police Department.

"They showed up and took our statements," Racheal recalls. "I sat down with a police artist, and they made a sketch, but that was the last we ever heard of it. They never caught the guy."

In June 2013, we presented Racheal Sajeski with two sets of mug shots taken of Otto Neil Nilson—one from his August 1974 arrest for assaulting the Gregg family and one from his 1975 arrest for the murder of Joan Kramer.

"That definitely looks like the guy with the gun," Racheal told us. "He was a little older, and his hair was thinner, but that definitely looks like him. I wish I could see a photo of him from the '80s." When we asked her how sure she was on a scale of one to ten, Racheal replied, "Eight."

At the time she was shown these photographs, Racheal was unaware that Nilson had used a high-powered rifle to instigate a hostage situation in September 1976.

If Racheal Sajeski is correct in her identification of Otto Neil Nilson being the man who showed up at her home with a rifle, that means the accused killer stalked both the Kramer and DePalma families in the years after the murders of Joan and Jeannette. For Nilson to have been the man at Racheal's doorstep, however, he would have had to break out of Trenton Psychiatric Hospital. Still, this remains entirely possible. Deep in the records room of the South Orange Police Department is a file folder containing the remnants of Otto Neil Nilson's criminal record. Inside of this folder is an undated index arrest card. The charge? "Escape." The complainant? "Trenton Psy Hosp."

For many years after, talk of the DePalma case calmed to a lull. The residents of Springfield and Mountainside were more than happy to forget the supposed Satanic murder that had occurred in the Houdaille Quarry, and once Jeannette's family moved out of the area, this task became even more achievable. However, when Mark Moran and Mark Sceurman printed the basic details of the case as related to them by the spooked shop owner in the May 2003 issue of *Weird NJ*, former Springfield residents with memories to share of the township's darkest hour began to creep out of the woodwork.

By this point in time, Sceurman and Moran had forgotten that the magazine had received and published a letter that vaguely referenced Jeannette only a few years before. In late 1997, *Weird NJ* received a letter from a fan named Billy Martin. The short letter, entitled "In the Watchung Mountains," read:

> *There was an alleged ritual sacrifice, I think, in the Houdaille Quarry near Springfield. A local dog brought a body part home to it's [sic] master which led to an investigation. I don't know if it is true or just a local myth…*

Martin's letter would later appear in *Weird NJ* Issue #9, released in October of that year. More letters would eventually grace the desks of the two editors. These new letters, however, all began to arrive in envelopes missing a return address. Some were sincere and helpful:

The Garden State's most unconventional tour guides: Mark Sceurman and Mark Moran. Their magazine, *Weird NJ*, rescued the DePalma case from obscurity in 2003. *Collection of the authors.*

You've only skimmed the surface. Everyone in the area knows about Gregg Sanders, but there was also a girl named Jeanette [sic] who was picked up while hitchhiking in Springfield, and was ritually murdered by a satanic cult…

If I remember correctly, she was a very, very religious girl and many felt that she was a target for Satanists. I can remember reading all about it in all the papers. Her name was Jeannette DePalma and she was found on an altar…

Jeannette lived in Springfield, her family lived on the top of the mountain, that is up Mountain View Road from Shunpike Road. When her body was found it was not on an alter [sic], there were logs around her body. Keep digging for information, she needs to be put to rest finally. Sorry I can't give you my name for more reasons than one but the information above is true.

Other letters were far more eccentric, to say the least:

Hi Mark,
Depalma. [sic] J? Jeanette? [sic] Joanne? 1971 or 1972, yawn. The Star Ledger was not even a SPERM. Try 1970 or 69. There were only two papers that serviced that part of Union County. The Newark Evening News *and the* Elizabeth Daily Journal. *But no one remembers Barringer High, in Newark. All they know is Malcholm Shabaz [sic]. So how can you expect someone to remember an unsolved case like this.*
   I'm tired, think I'll go back to bed.

Using these letters as a starting point, Sceurman and Moran began to dig through the microfilm archives held at the Elizabeth Public Library. The two were able to find all of the *Elizabeth Daily Journal's* coverage of the DePalma case. When we returned to those archives in 2012, we were shocked to find that the September 1972 microfilm reel had been deliberately damaged. An unidentified person had physically torn the last week of that month from the reel. This week contained the majority of the newspaper's coverage of Jeannette's murder and the only references to the Kramer murder to be found within articles pertaining to the DePalma case. Someone either wanted a grim souvenir of one of New Jersey's most infamous killings or did not want future sleuths to discover any connection to the murder of Joan Kramer. This mysterious thief had been so eager to steal the piece of preserved journalism that he had torn the reel's cardboard case in the process.

As 2003 rolled on, Sceurman and Moran received enough information to begin work on a long-form article detailing the DePalma case. Soon after the two began conducting interviews, they aroused the interest of the Springfield Police Department. "Shortly after the publication of these letters, we received a call from a detective at the Springfield Police Department," Moran later wrote in *Weird NJ*. "He said that he was looking for clues in the case of Jeannette DePalma, and wanted to know if *we* could help *him*! The detective told me that unsolved murder cases were never closed, and that the police had to track down any new leads that came their way. Apparently, someone brought an issue of *Weird NJ* to the attention of the police and they wanted to know the names of the people who had written the letters to us so that they could question them."

Moran explained to the detective that all of the letters were unsigned and contained no return address. The journalist then asked how much this detective actually knew about the case.

"Not too much," the detective replied. "All records prior to 1995 were destroyed due to flooding during Hurricane Floyd…"

The detective's story did not convince *Weird NJ*'s readers. "This has 'cover-up' written all over it," wrote one such subscriber.

> *I truly believe that whole excuse about the great deluge of '99 is completely ridiculous. Was Noah passing by in his arc? Those silly Springfield cops. Upper class people live in Springfield. The town doesn't have the money to maintain municiple* [sic] *buildings? Nice try. All that bullshit about Satanism is just a smoke screen to take the minds and attention of the people off of the truely* [sic] *guilty by creating a scare—or should I say scam?*

The DePalma family did not believe the Springfield Police Department's flood excuse either. "They always say that there was a flood," Jeannette's nephew John Bancey told *Weird NJ* in 2004. "Come on, that's bullshit. There's no more records? There's got to be records in the prosecutor's office."

During the preparation for this book, we sought an official response regarding the supposedly lost files. Open Public Records Act requests were sent to both the Springfield Police Department and the Union County

Three young Springfield residents playing in the street during a 1980 flood. This flood possibly destroyed Jeannette DePalma's original case file. *Photo by Ed Cardinal.*

Prosecutor's Office, each asking for a copy of the DePalma case file. After being told over the telephone that the office was enthusiastically considering releasing "most, if not all" of Jeannette's case file, we were later denied access to any and all of the requested records via e-mail:

> *Unfortunately, our Office is not going to waive the "criminal investigatory record" exemption under our OPRA statute for the records you seek on the Jeannette DePalma file. The decision was made for a variety of reasons. Most notably is the fact that the investigation is still open. We greatly appreciate your patience in affording us the time to review your request and reach a considered decision.*
>
> *If you have any questions, please let me know and I will attempt to answer them to the extent I am able to do so. By way of this email, our Office considers your request closed.*
> *SDAG/AAP ROBERT VANDERSTREET*
> *Union County Prosecutor's Office.*

Once the Springfield Police Department received our Open Public Records Act request, representatives once again claimed that the file had been destroyed in 1999, when Hurricane Floyd flooded much of Union County.

"That file was not destroyed during Hurricane Floyd," retired Springfield lieutenant Peter Hammer insists. "That file was missing all the way back in the mid-1980s. When I took over the Detective Bureau back around 1985, I asked for all of Springfield's cold case files so I could brush up. I was brought all but two case files: the Beverly Manoff file and the DePalma file. The evidence techs told me they couldn't find it."

Months later, in January 2014, we once again heard from Peter Hammer. "I was at the Springfield Police Department last December," Hammer wrote in an e-mail. "I hear that your research may have caused them to locate the case file and some other evidence that was stored in the attic of the old Girl Scout house. The Detective Bureau offices were located there, but not the evidence room. My guess is you rattled some cages…"

Armed with this new information, we sent another Open Public Records Act request to the Springfield Police Department, this time citing Hammer's e-mail. On January 29, 2014, Detective Lieutenant Judd A. Levenson replied with the following e-mail:

> *I have received the request that was recently sent to Chief of Police John Cook of the Springfield (NJ) Police Department. Request was for access to*

available documents pertaining to the death of Jeannette DePalma in 1972. The information you received from a retired police officer pertaining to this agency recently locating any evidence pursuant to this death investigation was not correct. As to police reports, this agency suffered a catastrophic loss of old police files when the police department went under 7 feet of water and raw sewage as a result of the serious flooding associated with Tropical Storm Floyd in September of 1999. Some police reports were recently located during the recent renovations of the police HQ in 2009– 2010. As this official cause of death determination made by the medical examiner's office is listed as "undetermined" this matter is considered to be classified the same as any unsolved homicide. Accordingly no reports held by this agency can be released. Furthermore, the current policy in Union County NJ is that the Union County Prosecutor's Office Homicide Unit is the primary investigative agency for all active and or unsolved homicides or suspicious or undetermined types of death cases and this agency therefore has no ability to release or grant access to any documents, even if this could be done, without the prior authorizatuion [sic] of the prosecutor's office. Pursuant to the NJ Open Public Records Act and the provisions of N.J.S.A. 47:1A-3.a, your request for any documents or access to documents is hereby denied for the aforementioned reasons.

Sincerely,
Detective Lieutenant Judd A. Levenson

"Judd may have thrown me under the bus for a good reason," Hammer says cryptically. "That department has had a lot of problems…"

"That is Judd Levenson's way of saying that he is not going to get involved in this," says Ed Kisch. "I can tell you about Judd and how he would react to things, and Judd would not delve into that case one iota. This was politics."

Kisch says he is used to fellow policemen dismissing their duties as law enforcement officers in order to further an ulterior agenda.

"In 1997, I attended a juvenile officers meeting," Kisch recalls. "By this time, I was a juvenile officer. Changes were being made to put the juvenile officers back on the Juvenile Conference Committee. This was mandated by the state of New Jersey. The juvenile officers were to act as advisors to this committee in the event that they had any questions about an accused juvenile and his or her actions. An assistant Union County prosecutor who attended this meeting felt that if any juvenile officers were allowed onto this committee, it could be a detriment to any juvenile sitting before them if he or she was asked and admitted to other crimes. This assistant prosecutor's opinion was that the only way that the juvenile officers could be in the room was if they 'left their badges at the door.' If anyone at this meeting would not agree to this, it would be a deal breaker in regards to the juvenile officers being put back on the committee. Being the cop that I am, I immediately spoke up and said, 'Well, I guess this is a deal breaker.' I took an oath to uphold the laws in the state of New Jersey; nowhere did it say that I could pick and choose when to investigate any crimes admitted to me or in my presence. Let me tell you something—the badge *never* comes off."

EPILOGUE

S tanding on the Devil's Teeth today, it is hard not to imagine the countless people who have stood here before, staring at the rusted-out trucks and Quonset hut below, completely unaware that they were standing on the site of a supposed ritual sacrifice.

The Houdaille Quarry is now owned by the State of New Jersey. When we visited the site in 2014, we were met by gun-wielding Union County police officers. Despite this heightened police presence, the abandoned quarry and its surrounding woods remain a haven for Springfield's homeless population. The sleeping bags, discarded empty food cans and soda bottles that can be found throughout those woods are a testament to this. The area is littered with many other curiosities—faded pull-tab beer cans, a thirty-year-old Sucrets tin, an infant's tattered sweater.

The quarry now looks slightly different than it did in 1972. For one, the area has become much more densely wooded. "I am not advocating the desecration of forested woodland," Ed Cardinal says, "but I would bet that if you cut any one of those trees down, you would find less than forty-three rings in them."

Yet in spite of their age, the echoes of the last four decades seem to be held within these trees.

In June 1989, John List was finally apprehended after seventeen years on the run. He had been living in Colorado and Virginia under the name Bob Clark and had even remarried. He was eventually tried for the murders of his family and found guilty. During List's trial, Dr. Steven Simring, who had previously diagnosed Otto Neil Nilson as a paranoid schizophrenic, testified that List had murdered his family as the result of a "mid-life crisis." Sentenced to life in prison, List died on March 21, 2008. His body lay unclaimed in a Middlesex County morgue for some time before finally being interred beside his mother in Frankenmuth, Michigan. Killer and victim finally reunited in death.

The charred remains of the List home were demolished in September 1972. Truckloads of blackened debris were being hauled off as Jeannette DePalma's body was being lowered from the Devil's Teeth, only three miles away.

Otto Neil Nilson died on March 2, 1992. Acquaintances of his recall being told that the fifty-seven-year-old former accountant had taken his own life. Some claim that he was actually murdered by a fellow patient while confined to Trenton Psychiatric Hospital, while others maintain that he merely succumbed to a heart ailment. We could not locate any record of a final resting place for Nilson. We were also unable to find a single solved or unsolved homicide in the State of New Jersey that even vaguely resembled the murders of Jeannette DePalma, Joan Kramer or Mary Ann Pryor and Lorraine Kelly in the years following Nilson's committal.

Nancy Pryor still lives in New Jersey and actively pursues any available information related to her sister's unsolved murder. In June 2013, we contacted Sergeant Russell Christiana of the Bergen County Prosecutor's Office regarding the homicides of Mary Ann Pryor and Lorraine Kelly. During the conversation, we detailed the similarities between the Pryor/Kelly case and the cases of Jeannette DePalma and Joan Kramer, along with the criminal activities of Otto Neil Nilson. Sergeant Christiana agreed that the cases were all "very similar" and that he would further investigate Nilson. As of 2015, Christiana is no longer assigned to the Pryor/Kelly case, and the Bergen County Prosecutor's Office did not respond to questions regarding any possible investigation of Nilson.

On Wednesday, July 9, 2014, Darlene Bancey vanished from the Lakewood Personal Care Home in Monroe County, Pennsylvania, where she had been living. Her body was found in a lake behind the facility early the next morning. A coroner later ruled that Bancey had died as a result of drowning. According to her family, the autopsy also detected in her system the presence of medication that had not been prescribed to her. An investigation later revealed a history of safety and emergency training violations at the personal care home. Fire drills had not been properly performed by Lakewood staff, and an incident where two residents violently assaulted each other went unreported in January of that year. Bancey died only one week before a previously scheduled second interview with us was going to take place.

Sam Calabrese, once in charge of the DePalma investigation as a detective sergeant with the Springfield Police Department, died on December 8, 2014, having successfully avoided answering a single question regarding the death of the young girl.

The Union County Prosecutor's Office has been aware of Rose MacNaughton's letter regarding Mike A. and his possible involvement in the murder of Jeannette DePalma for over a decade. At no point during this period of time did any detective or representative contact Ms. MacNaughton in order to investigate Mike A. further. Inquiries we sent regarding which investigator is currently handling the DePalma case have gone ignored.

Despite these setbacks, independent investigators and armchair detectives continue to research the DePalma case in the hopes that a resolution will soon be reached. Some argue that the case has never been closer to being solved. However, with the Springfield Police Department and the Union County Prosecutor's Office continuing to remain silent after four decades of perceived indifference and deception, it is easy to see why others do not share the same optimism. Still, significant developments have been made, and new pieces of information continue to be slowly revealed by those who remember the girl on the mountain.

While murmurs of Mike A.'s reputed interest in the occult now swirl in the ether, one is left to wonder whether it is once again conceivable that Jeannette DePalma actually *was* murdered by devil worshippers.

It is certainly possible. But then again, isn't everything else?

With the profound lack of concrete information regarding her final hours on earth, the list of possibilities definitely rivals the list of impossibilities. Perhaps Jeannette DePalma was doomed to forever be the vague warning that parents, both present and future, would give to their kids:

Don't talk to strangers.
Don't hitchhike.
Don't go into the woods.
Look what happened to Jeannette DePalma…

A cautionary tale for paranoid suburbanite families everywhere.

ABOUT THE AUTHORS

Jesse P. Pollack was born and raised in the Garden State and has served as a contributing writer for *Weird NJ* magazine since 2001. Also an accomplished musician, Pollack's soundtrack work has been heard on *Driving Jersey*, an Emmy-nominated PBS documentary series. He is married with two children. *Death on the Devil's Teeth* is his first book.

Mark Moran graduated from Parsons School of Design in New York City, where he studied fine art, illustration and photography. In the early 1990s, Moran teamed up with Mark Sceurman to create *Weird NJ* magazine, the ultimate travel guide to the Garden State's local legends and best-kept secrets. The magazine has since spawned several books and a History Channel television series. Moran lives with his wife and their two daughters in suburban New Jersey.